One Thousand Days
in Hong Kong

One Thousand Days in Hong Kong

M. V. Harland

麥　克　蘭

Mark Harland

© Mark Harland 2017

Published by MVH Publishing

A CIP catalogue record for this book is available from the British Library.

ISBN 978-0-9935895-3-9 (ePub)
ISBN 978-0-9935895-4-6 (mobi)
ISBN 978-0-9935895-5-3 (Hardback)
ISBN 978-0-9935895-6-0 (Hardback)

Book layout and design by Clare Brayshaw

Prepared and printed by:

York Publishing Services Ltd
64 Hallfield Road
Layerthorpe
York
YO31 7ZQ

Tel: 01904 431213

Website: www.yps-publishing.co.uk

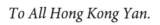

To All Hong Kong Yan.

FOREWORD

I have never been one to keep a diary, or been much of a photographer, so this book is written largely from a memory that I inherited from my maternal grandfather, a Yorkshireman called Walter Jewitt. Grandad was a superb gardener and also a cricket buff. He could remember tomato crop yields and match scores and details going back many years without the slightest difficulty so I guess it is his genes that I have to be thankful for when I write this book some five decades after the events occurred.

One of my favourite authors is James Clavell and when some twenty years ago I finally got around to reading *Noble House* it took me back in a time machine to the Hong Kong that I knew in the Sixties. The British Crown Colony of Hong Kong, as it was then known, was a gentler land than it is today. The formal handover to the Communist Chinese Government in Beijing, or Peking as it was then called, was thirty years away and nobody gave it the slightest thought. The Island of Hong Kong had been ceded to Britain in perpetuity by the 1842 Treaty of Nanking and it was only the New Territories acquired on a ninety-nine year lease in 1898 that needed to be given back, as it were. Or so we thought.

In 1966 the summer seemed to be endless, England had just won the World Cup and what was left of the Empire was thriving in commercial terms. Millionaires of every nationality under the sun were created in Hong Kong where a combination of British administration and laissez-faire economics created the richest city on earth per capita. Over the border to the north however, where the Cultural Revolution was inspired by the Communist Party Chairman, Mao Tse-Tung, things were not well. People were starving in many parts of the country, the peasants were revolting and Mao's Red Guards imposed civil order in the most brutal fashion.

In Hong Kong we hardly bothered to take even a cursory glance northwards. Life was good, even for those who lived in lowly circumstances having fled from the poverty and tyranny of Mao's China. These then are my recollections of those thousand days.

CHAPTER 1

Nothing prepares you for the assault on your senses when you arrive in Hong Kong. Arriving on a steaming hot August night by cargo-liner into the middle of Victoria Harbour, the 'Fragrant Harbour,' was an amazing experience. Looking back we were lucky. Most British families arrived in Hong Kong in those days after a gruelling thirty-six hour flight on a Bristol Britannia turboprop airliner. We had the luxury of twenty eight days at sea including three days in Singapore which had given us a taste of the Orient en route as it were.

We had voyaged on the s.s. *Bendoran* a Leith registered vessel of about eleven thousand tons and had probably averaged about sixteen knots instead of a Britannia's three hundred. Consequently we were acclimatised and not jet lagged, having wound our clocks forward an hour on no less than seven separate occasions. Friends and colleagues of Dad's met us on board for drinks before we officially disembarked. They included my old school pal from Malta days, Mike Davis and his father Bob. We were soon chatting away and Mike told me how good the school was and how pretty some of the girls were in 'our' class.

'You will be in Class 3A won't you, Mark? You passed your Eleven Plus so you're bound to be. There's Sally, Diana, Annette and....'

Mike had obviously gone into skirt mode a bit earlier than me. I was wondering, and hoping, if the school had a decent cricket pitch not how many girls would be in my class.

Shortly before midnight we were all asked to formally disembark *Bendoran* which had been our home and haven for over four weeks. We said goodbye to our fellow passengers, promising to meet up again in the months ahead. In reality we only regularly kept contact with one of them, a wonderful Irish Salesian priest called Patrick Corcoran. I will write more about that wonderful man later.

The *Bendoran* had docked alongside Number 3 berth in Kowloon on the mainland opposite Hong Kong Island. Travelling in friends' cars we drove north about a mile to the Kowloon terminal of the Hongkong Yaumatei Ferry Co. At a signal from a loadmaster our cars were driven up ramps onto the upper vehicle deck of a large double-ended ferry which had the ability to sail in either direction which saved it having to turn around when docking. This was exciting stuff. Within two hours of docking on one vessel I was already at sea on another albeit much smaller. With the ferry under way and heading for the Island terminal about two miles to the south I got out of the car onto the deck and surveyed the scene before my eyes. It was mind boggling. My driver and 'guide' was a chap called Cyril Hatton, a colleague of Dad's who had been stationed in Hong Kong for a year already and he knew the ropes. 'Squirrel' as Dad called him was keen to point out places, features and landmarks to me during the twenty minute journey. He was waving his arms here, there and everywhere.

'On your left that's the Yau Ma Tei typhoon shelter. That's the Peak at the top of the mountain there. There's a Star Ferry over there-look! And there's another one going the other way. That's the clock tower to your left, there! That's the new Ocean Terminal there – look!'

It was almost too much to take in. What was a typhoon shelter for? It looked empty to me just like an empty dock – all harbour moles and no boats. The clock tower instantly reminded me of the one in Aden that we had left about five thousand miles behind. There was a large white liner berthed on the south side of the Ocean Terminal, probably of the American President Lines, and frequent visitors from their base-port in California some six thousand miles away. And everywhere you looked there were cargo ships of every size and description. Without exception they were surrounded by lighters loading and unloading cargo and it was about one 'o' clock in the morning. I just couldn't take in all in. Doesn't anybody go to bed here? As we neared the terminal on Hong Kong Island Squirrel's arms were still in windmill fashion. Maybe he'd been a semaphore expert in the Navy because I knew that, like Dad, he had also been in the Andrew – a sailor's slang for the Royal Navy. He wasn't going to stop this chap but it was all good stuff.

'There, look, that's the P & O Building....there's HMS Tamar the naval base....the Old Post Office and.....crikey we're nearly there....back into the car, Mark.'

I took particular notice when Squirrel had mentioned the naval base. Dad's father, Pop to me, had been stationed in Hong Kong and the China Station when he himself had been an Electrical Artificer (First Class) before the First World War. He had told us that he just loved Hong Kong and in fact had volunteered for two separate two year stints. Just before we had left London a month earlier he had regaled me with tales of the six week voyage each way on a battleship. I couldn't wait to see where he might have been based.

The drive from the ferry terminal to our hotel, the Sunning House in Causeway Bay, took about twenty minutes. It must have getting on for one thirty in the morning but there were people absolutely everywhere. I had never seen so many people in my life. The pavements were full of people. The shops were full of people and even the roads seemed full of people. Squirrel seemed to be sounding the car horn every few seconds. And boy was it hot and humid! Cars didn't have air conditioning in those days and both the car's front windows were open to the maximum. We stopped at a traffic light in a district called Wanchai and then, via the open window, I had my first experience of it. A hawker carrying fruit or something in baskets balanced on both ends of a long shoulder slung bamboo pole rasped his throat for what seemed an eternity and spat the contents out straight ahead of him onto the pavement. I cringed.

'Yuck! That's disgusting.'

'You'll get used to it Mark. It's the norm out here. In a few weeks you won't even notice it.'

'Squirrel' was right. Welcome to Hong Kong! Ten minutes later we pulled up outside the Sunning House which was to be our home for the next six weeks at least. Mum, Dad and sister arrived in other friend's cars and taxis soon after. Luggage, in fact a considerable consignment of it, was taken to our two rooms on the sixth floor by coolies, and the adults repaired to the bar for drinks. I had never been up so late in my life and it was probably 2 a.m. before we retired.

I was awoken shortly after 7 a.m. by a road drill right outside my bedroom window. It was only just light I remember. The hum of *Bendoran*'s marine turbines had been almost therapeutic but this was bedlam. I opened the window intending to give the origin of these excessive decibels a piece of my mind. Two things stopped me – the heat and the smell. I hadn't noticed either the night before but now it was just awful. I slammed the window shut and tried to go back to sleep. I failed.

We had a late breakfast in the large dining room and I was surprised to find ordinary English fayre like cornflakes, toast and marmalade. Quite what I had expected I'm not sure. Tea was brought to the table in silver pots that were incredibly hot and waiters brought us little mittens to use. There were no tea bags either and proper strainers were provided.

Breakfast over I wanted to immediately walk out and explore but was quickly hailed back by Dad who told me that his pal Maurice, who had met us on the ship the night before, was coming to take us out to Stanley where he and his wife Joyce and daughter Susan lived. It was to be our first real sight of Hong Kong in daylight. Sure enough it wasn't long before 'Moss' pulled up in his Mark II Jaguar. Twenty five years year later when watching the *Inspector Morse* TV series it reminded of those early days in Hong Kong. Dad sat in the front with Moss and Mum, sister and me in the back. It was already very hot indeed, probably about thirty degrees Celsius. And the humidity was just suffocating. Within a few minutes our shirts were wet through with perspiration. Ventilation was provided by a through current of warm air via small triangular corner windows known as quarter lights. They were also disposal vents for the ash and dog ends of innumerable cigarettes smoked by both Dad and Moss in equal measure. Nothing had changed much in that department since our days in Malta six years earlier although Dad had converted from the almost radioactive Senior Service to Rothmans if my memory serves me correctly. Moss was still a Piccadilly fan.

The Jag turned right out of Hysan Avenue into a very busy road called Leighton Road and within seconds Moss braked hard to avoid a tram turning right out of Percival Street. The tram driver sounded a loud bell and probably shrieked an unpleasant Cantonese epithet or two.

'Bloody trams have always got right of way here, Vic. You've gotta watch 'em. They can't leave the tracks of course but they stop and start whenever they feel like it.'

Dad was not fond of driving in heavy traffic. He never had been. I could sense already that he was not looking forward to driving on Hong Kong's teeming roads when our family car arrived from the importing agent. That would not be for a few more days yet so perhaps he could acclimatise to the local conditions as a passenger first and at least get his bearings. Some hope!

We headed roughly west through busy streets with shops spilling out their wares over all pavements. There were hawkers everywhere selling fruit and peelings and skins seemed to be everywhere. The smell through the open car windows was pungent, accentuated of course by the omnipresent heat. We started to climb into a less built up area and passed a Sikh temple on our left just before some traffic lights at a major intersection. When the lights turned green we turned sharp left into a hill called Stubbs Road and kept climbing...and climbing...and climbing. The road twisted and turned sometimes through a deep cutting in the reddish local rock which at first glance could be mistaken for sandstone but which was in fact decomposed granite. In a short while a vista opened to our left and we looked down several hundred feet onto a bright green racetrack complete with viewing stadia. Moss was keen to act as a guide.

'That's the famous Happy Valley racecourse. You should see it on race days. It is absolutely packed with thousands of spectators. In the summer the meetings are usually in the evenings after sunset when the temperature dips a little.'

What I didn't learn until quite a while later was that everyday gambling was illegal in Hong Kong and that the on course 'Tote' was the only place in the Colony you could actually place a bet. Hence the huge crowds of locals attending to at least partially slake the urge to gamble that is endemic in all Chinese. We kept climbing and passed blocks of flats on our right hand side. At the time they seemed towering, probably about eight stories. Building land was already at a premium in crowded Hong Kong and looking back it reminds me of the tune 'The only way is up, baby' by Otis Clay but it would be another fourteen years before it was even written. Moss continued with his commentary.

'You see those really tall buildings just up from the racecourse? Well in the morning before it gets too hot many of the racehorses are often exercised on the flat roofs by the trainers and stable boys.'

Yeah right. Moss always liked to pull my leg, ever since I was a small boy in Malta. Eventually we reached some sort of a plateau and what looked like several acres of flat land to our left was being prepared for building work. A sign portrayed an artist's impression of a new Girl Guides HQ. Lucky girls. This was prime building land. Surely they weren't going to take up all of it? The road started to go downhill and suddenly the vista changed. Ahead of us to the south was the South China Sea and it looked absolutely stunning as it shimmered in the morning sunshine. The road was called Wong Nei Chong Gap Road and it was probably the first truly Chinese name that I managed to get my tongue round. Just as Stubbs Road had meandered up hill so this one snaked downhill. There was mountainside to our left covered in lush vegetation and this being the rainy season every so often you could see man-made nullahs or drains carrying rainwater safely under the road rather than cascading across it. Some of the boulders were enormous and those that posed the biggest danger to traffic by protruding out too far were painted white to warn drivers of wider vehicles. On the way down hill we passed a No. 6 bus coming uphill and Moss kept the Jag well to the left to avoid clipping his offside. It did cross my mind at the time that if two buses met on a narrow bend there might not be enough room. In any event the chances of travelling by bus on this route were not high. Mark the eternal optimist, again.

'That's the bus from Stanley into town. We always drive though when going into town shopping. Joyce doesn't like buses. Tell you what, we've got time so let's stop in Deep Water Bay for a cooling drink shall we?'

After going steadily downhill for about two miles we reached an intersection overlooking the sea and turned sharp right, the road dropping right down to sea level within a couple of hundred yards. To my amazement on the right was a large piece of flat land which was the home of Deep Water Bay Golf Club with its nine hole course. Nobody was playing. It was far too hot. To our left was a nice if small beach and within a short distance the Jaguar pulled up at a refreshments kiosk complete with shading umbrellas and chairs. It reminded me of our days in Malta with Coke and 7 Up adverts everywhere but what was this? San Miguel? Moss ordered two 'San Migs' one each for him and Dad and soft drinks for me, Linda and Mum. I would have liked a beer too but my initiation with malted hops instigated on the *Bendoran* courtesy of Father Paddy had been our little secret and this was neither the time nor the place for a confession. I stuck to Coke.

It was hot. Boy was it hot. Moss obviously fancied himself as the Michael Fish of his day.

'It's not the heat here, Vic. It's the humidity. Actually it's not as hot as Malta but it feels worse because of the 'relative humidity' which sticks to around ninety-five percent from May to October.'

The relative humidity? That was a new one on me despite the fact I was savvy meteorologically speaking. Or so I thought. I would have to wait for a day or so to hear my first weather report on Radio Hong Kong before I could claim full comprehension. I remember one or two Europeans lying on the beach but otherwise it looked very quiet. With the exception of the shade provided by the beach umbrellas there was no escaping the high, fierce sun. At about twenty two degrees north we were just inside the tropics after all. The Tropic of Cancer in our case.

After about a half an hour we got back into the Jag and headed south for Stanley. Rejoining the main Island Road at the previously mentioned intersection we turned right and headed south for Repulse Bay. I noticed a particularly large and picturesque house to the right perched on a cliff edge with its own swimming pool. It had a castle-like turret and must have cost a fortune to build with the civil engineering involved given its precarious position. Several years later when watching the film *Love is a many splendoured thing* I recognised it immediately. The road continued its winding way down to sea level and the Bay itself. The beautiful beach to our right was wide and deserted. To our left were several large blocks of attractive flats and in the middle of all of them was the famous Repulse Bay Hotel. It was Victorian Colonial architecture at its finest. The road started to climb again and the drop to our right towards the sea became greater and greater. There were only rocks and some vegetation between the road and the sea at the bottom and by the time we got to the top the drop must have been several hundred feet. About halfway up another No. 6 bus came screaming downhill at about fifty miles an hour.

'It's downhill all the way to Stanley now' added Moss. 'Joyce will have a bit of lunch ready for us.'

The scenery to the first time viewer was amazing. The bright green hillsides covered in lush green trees at the height of a hot, wet and humid summer contrasted with the blue of the South China Sea that shimmered like a million mirrors. It was probably about midday with the sun at its zenith as we approached a well sign posted roundabout. Straight on for Tai Tam and right for Stanley. The turn complete the sea was now on our left and I noticed a small but pretty beach called Hairpin Beach maybe fifty feet below us. It too was deserted. The road twisted and turned past pretty houses and bungalows with the occasional block of flats, none more than three storeys high. Bougainvillaea and jacaranda trees were everywhere and one tree beside some flats called Country Apartments was a mass of bright red flowers.

'That's called a Flame of the Forest. Some of our Boys live there. Really nice flats.'

Our Boys was Moss speak for work colleagues who also worked for the same Government organisation. We passed a road to our left called Stanley Mound road which looked like it led down to yet another beach. A petrol station on our right sported the famous sea shell logo and the banner Shellubrication. It caught me by surprise. Was I really expecting Ying Tong Petroluem? Maybe I'd been listening to the Goons too much. Going downhill we rounded another sharp bend and then turned right into Carmel Road, named after a Carmelite Convent that took up an enormous amount of space. Apart from the building itself it was surrounded by about an acre of gardens. The Jag slowed and we turned into a private steep drive with car parking slots angled herringbone style. We pulled into one with a number six painted in white on the concrete.

'This is it. Welcome to Gordon Terrace folks. This is where we live.'

Gordon Terrace was in fact three quite separate blocks each of six flats and only three storeys high. The blocks were set in a semi-circle with a grass circle in the middle and in the centre was an old fashioned green iron street light that would not have looked out of place in any English town at the time. The other half of the semi-circle faced south over the convent, Stanley Market, another green hill about a mile away and then beyond that once again to the South China Sea. It was bewitching and magnificent at the same time.

Moss, Joyce and their daughter Susan lived in the middle block facing almost exactly due south. Joyce was on the balcony on the second floor and waving to us. We walked up four flights of stairs to be greeted and shown inside. We had cold drinks on the balcony and just chilled out. A large electric fan whirled continuously as it traversed through about a hundred and twenty degrees of azimuth every fifteen seconds. If the view from the car park had been good then the view from the balcony was even more spectacular. The added height accentuated the visibility and looking beyond the hill a mile away I could just make out some islands probably fifteen miles distant. I didn't realise that Hong Kong's territory extended that far. In fact it didn't as I was to rudely find out the following summer.

'That's Stanley Fort barracks on that hill up there Vic. You can't really see it from here but when you get up there it's a massive piece of land. There's a good NAAFI too for shopping.'

I thought it was a bit of an odd name, Stanley Fort. Why not Fort Stanley? We had a Fort William, a Fort George, a Fort Rosalie and so on. Very odd. Maybe a Victorian cartographer had had one too many in the midday sun or was dyslexic? There's a reason for everything. Anyway Stanley Fort it was. Moss told us that it was currently garrisoned by the 1st Battalion the Welch Regiment.

After a light salad lunch (tinned salmon I think from memory) Moss picked up the phone to place a grocery order with a store in the village called, appropriately, Stanley Stores. He reeled off a whole number of items from a written list and then almost as an afterthought added 'oh yes and twelve bottles of San Mig and two hundred Piccadilly.' It was that last bit that amused me. Fancy putting cigarettes on a grocery order.

'We'll give them ten minutes, Marcus, then we'll go down in the car to pick up the order.'

Sure enough I was soon back in a stinking hot car again which was probably over a hundred degrees inside by now as Moss had forgotten to put the rattan mat over the windscreen to shield it from the sun. We drove out past the convent and downhill just a couple of hundred yards before turning into a narrow road that led to a fruit and veg market. Stanley Stores was up a flight of steps to our left and after parking the Jag we trotted up the steps. I was most impressed. There were chest freezers everywhere, shelves loaded with bottles and tins and crates of beer stacked up three or four deep. Did everybody drink a lot out here? I saw glass cabinets with several different brands of brandy too which surprised me. Who drank all that lot? Our order was ready, packed into a large cardboard box which I carried down the steps. Moss carried the beer. We got to within about twenty yards of the car when Moss suddenly froze. We couldn't believe what we saw. A Chinese bloke, probably in his thirties, was stood in front of the Jag's bonnet and doing his damndest to prise off the metal leaping cat that was the manufacturer's emblem. Chink had picked the wrong bloke to annoy. Moss put the crate of beer on the pavement, took a last drag of his fag and started his run up like he was taking a penalty. His right foot landed in the Chinamen's arse so hard it lifted him right onto the bonnet. He turned and ran off, no doubt with a bruise to arrive the following day. It would have hurt too. Like most of his colleagues Moss always wore long socks with highly polished brown shoes with toe caps. When I related the tale to Dad later he laughed loudly and told me that Moss had been a very nimble right back in his day when he played for the Scarborough Wireless Station football team. Moss had been born near Middlesbrough and had followed the Club all his life. Were he alive today he would be very proud of them indeed.

'That's the only way to deal with these people, Marcus' were the only words he had to say.

Today he would probably get arrested and charged with violating the victim's human rights and banged up. Not so in colonial Hong Kong. Quite right too. Up the Empire! On a wet winter's afternoon and if with nothing much on the agenda I will often go to my box set of thirty-three Inspector Morse DVDs and pick one out for two hours of superb entertainment. The sight of Morse's Mk II Jag always reminds me of that time with Moss at Stanley Market and the Chinaman with the sore arse.

'Dew lei lo mo' were the only words the miscreant shouted as he limped into the fruit market never to be seen again. It would be a while before I learnt what that Cantonese epithet actually meant.

Moss checked the car's mascot which appeared intact and with another Piccadilly already lit all was well with world. Five minutes later we were back in the flat where

Mum and Joyce were still talking nineteen to the dozen. The only words I remember went something like this:

'The flat at No. 8 will be vacant in October, Hylda. It would be lovely if you all lived in Stanley too.'

Just before dusk we were back at the Sunning House Hotel, having taken the same route backwards, so to speak. So ended the first of a thousand days in Hong Kong. Wow!

CHAPTER 2

Over the course of the next week we settled into the Sunning House and 'got our bearings' so to speak. We had two big rooms on the sixth floor overlooking Hysan Avenue and the Lee Gardens Hotel immediately opposite. In a few days' time our new car would arrive but in the meantime we explored the immediate area on foot. It was quite simply mind boggling. No matter what time of day you ventured out the streets seemed to teem with people of all ages. What immediately struck me was the huge numbers of schoolchildren all in uniform with crisp white shirts and blouses and all seemingly carrying old fashioned satchels slung over their shoulders. None of them seemed to be on school holidays like we still were. We walked up Percival Street following the tram lines and noticed a smart cinema on the corner called the Lee. The billboard over the main entrance announced that the film currently showing was the recently released *Born Free* starring Virginia McKenna. We didn't know it at the time but we would make many visits to the Lee over the course of the next two months. Every other shop in Percival Street seemed to be a bookshop with piles of what looked like school textbooks not just in the shops but spilling out onto the pavements too. The trams seemed to be running every few minutes and all of them seemed to be heading in the direction of Happy Valley according to the destination window at the top of the front of every tram. This was repeated in Chinese characters underneath which of course we didn't understand at all. Occasionally a tram went past with no visible destination and we soon discovered that these were empty trams heading for the depot which was just around the corner in Canal Road. To defect off the main track a large lever had to be pulled which was sited on the pavement adjacent to the points like an old fashioned railway. The driver would stop, jump out, and pull the lever and then drive around the bend before stopping again, alighting and then resetting the points so that trams following him would end up heading for Happy Valley and not an early lunch in the depot. At the time it reminded me in a funny sort of way of my Hornby Doublo trainset. I already knew that Hong Kong did have its own railway but it would be a couple of months before I experienced it. After all I did have almost three years ahead of me.

Getting used to the new currency, and thus shopping, took a little time. There were sixteen Hong Kong dollars to the pound sterling which didn't make mental conversions very easy until one day Moss gave us sound advice.

'All you have to do is think that there are two dollars to a half-crown. Easy right?'

It was too and come to think of it we should have cottoned on to this way of thinking much earlier as during our three day stopover in Singapore there had been eight Straits dollars to the pound and thus a dollar was exactly half a crown. You try explaining that to a British school kid today. No way José or whatever the in phrase is today. Anyway to cut it short one's Hong Kong dollars seemed to stretch a long way. Everything seemed to be extraordinarily cheap whether it was an ice cream from the 'popsi man' (a mobile ice cream vendor with a scooter and refrigerated side car) or a newspaper. Cigarettes were almost given away at two dollars a pack. Little wonder that Moss had nonchalantly added 'and two hundred Piccadilly' onto the grocery order. A copy of the main English daily the South China Morning Post was thirty cents, the HK Tiger Standard twenty cents and the China Mail and the Star were both ten cents. I had been an avid newspaper reader since I was about seven so I was in heaven with these prices. You could buy a copy of all four papers for the equivalent of less than a shilling in old money.

The shops were amazing and to add to the incredible number of bookshops were others selling just rice all displayed in barrels with different price labels for the different types and varieties. Until then I thought that rice was just rice. The vast majority of rice consumed in Hong Kong was imported, not just from over the border in China but from Vietnam, Laos, the Philippines and Thailand although the deteriorating military situation in Indo-China was causing much disruption to supplies from the first two producers. We had already experienced a little of that a couple of weeks earlier when our ship the *s.s. Bendoran* travelling almost due north some one hundred miles off the coast of what was then South Vietnam was buzzed by a pair of US Air Force jets. No doubt we had been picked up on radar and they came out to take a look at us. The conflict in that part of the world would deteriorate sharply later but that is something I will expand on when my memories touch on early the following year.

The plethora of butchers shops were an education. By day they seemed to be fairly quiet but after dark they positively came alive. Duck seemed to be the most popular choice for customers and literally hundreds of them were cooked by every shop every day. We called it 'duck mangle' as they all seemed to have been rolled almost flat before being glazed in honey, cooked and then hung up on wires that looked like a bizarre washing line. The smell however was quite sublime. Pork was the other meat of choice in the main and although some was locally produced ninety percent of it was imported by rail from China. This was something that I was to see for myself within a couple of weeks.

When you reached the northern end of Percival Street you met the junction with a far wider and busier avenue called Hennessy Road. Unlike Percival Street, which was one-way, this was as wide a road as you will get in urban Hong Kong. It was four lanes wide (two in each direction) plus a double tram line (one in each direction) down the central reservation. Except there was no central reservation other than the odd tram stop which was raised about a foot above road level. The road is permanent bedlam from about seven in the morning until about midnight. At night every shop and building is just a blaze of neon lights, most of them in Chinese characters, advertising everything from cameras to massage parlours. In addition to trams and thousands of cars there were umpteen buses sporting the red and white livery of the China Motor Bus Company. They were mostly double- deckers as the single deckers were kept for the more rural routes with steep hills. We had already seen them in action on the road to Stanley. Those heading east were going to North Point, Shau Ki Wan and Chai Wan. Those heading west were going to Wanchai, Central, Kennedy Town and Western. At last a destination that made geographical sense.

To kill time in the evenings we would spend many hours in one of three huge department stores – Wing On, China Products and Daimaru. The first was a publicly quoted local enterprise, the second was wholly owned by the communist Chinese Government and the third was the Hong Kong branch of a mega Japanese department store. As a consequence they were all quite different and each had a character of their own. They were all a huge contrast to the Woolworths and Co-Ops of our native English stores. Apart from the vast array of different goods on display what struck me about the two Chinese stores was the smell of camphor, soaps and moth balls. There were lots of goods I had never seen before like carved figurines made from jade, soapstone and ivory. Yes ivory. In those days elephants were fair game and animal conservation was simply unheard of. People with money could have made an absolute fortune by investing in ivory in the Sixties but who could possibly have predicted the future? Jade was abundant and there were dragons, human figurines, fish and other animals all on display ranging in size from a few inches tall to a few feet. I was to learn that the buying of jade, mostly imported from Burma, was a risky business for the buyer. Regular auctions were held of rocks and boulders known to contain jade which the prospective buyer was invited to inspect before placing his bid. The problem was that the quantity and quality of the jade in the rock was not always indicated by what was visible on the outside and thus it was possible to buy a teaser or a bargain. Much jade sold in Hong Kong was in fact nephrite not jadeite so 'caveat emptor' was the name of the game. We bought lots of shirts, shorts and white socks more suited to the Tropics than much of the attire we had brought with us. We already had an inkling of what the required school uniform was. Summer drill for boys was navy blue shorts, white shirts (tucked into the shorts without fail), long white knee length socks and black laced shoes. For the girls it was pleated cotton dresses with brown shoes. The boys were all going to look like Sea Cadets despite the school being run by the Army.

And speaking of school Dad soon received a chit in his pigeon hole at work advising him of an Open Afternoon for all new kids starting the new term in September. It was the usual bullshit: 'The Headmaster and Staff invite you to an afternoon of...blah blah blah...'

Yes, Dad had actually started work despite the fact that we were still living in a hotel. His 'office' was the Composite Signals Organisation Station at a place called Little Sai Wan on the water's edge as you approached Hong Kong harbour from the east through the Lei Yue Mun Channel, the gap that separates the Island from the mainland. Our Salesian friend, Paddy, had pointed it out to Dad from the deck of *Bendoran* on the evening of our arrival but there was so much to take in it probably didn't register. Our car had still not arrived which in retrospect was probably a blessing as Dad was still 'getting his bearings' and Squirrel's verbal advice on navigating the best route had probably gone in one ear and out the other. So he was picked up at the hotel on his work days by colleagues on the same shift pattern. The most direct route involved first getting onto the aforementioned Hennessy Road, a task easier said than done with Percival Street being one-way not to mention the lethality of the trams. The distance to 'Sai Wan' as we all called it was probably only some four miles as the crow flies but in Hong Kong this is just wishful thinking. The road journey is via totally built up areas until you fork right at a place called Chai Wan (not to be confused with Wan Chai which must be a nightmare for dyslexics) and then go uphill for about a mile, appropriately past Paddy's Salesian School. At the top you turn left and start to descend past a huge civilian cemetery, a World War II military cemetery and a quarry where you see dozens of headstones being chipped and carved by the roadside. You wonder if you are heading for another planet as the road narrows between large boulders and descends again towards sea level. Of all things to come across is an English style traffic light which is controlled from the guard house at the entrance to 'Sai Wan' half a mile further down. Assuming a green light you continue down the hill until, rounding a bend, you see a military or border post style barrier across the road. Welcome to Little Sai Wan, the main listening post in the Far East of the UK's GCHQ – Government Communications Headquarters. If you think this place was the Bletchley Park of Asia with Nissen huts and pots of tea being brewed on coke fired stoves think again. I will tell you more later.

One Saturday morning the Davis's car turned up outside the hotel and I recognised the blue Ford Zodiac instantly. Did I want to go with them to the New Territories for the day? You bet I did. I was told to grab my swimming togs as with luck we might be able to use the pool at the Army barracks at a place called Sek Kong. We headed for the HYF vehicular ferry in town and we followed the route across the harbour in the reverse course to which I had travelled with Squirrel when we first arrived. There was another huge liner tied up at the Ocean Terminal on Kowloon side and another vessel was berthed, I think where had been *Bendoran* and it was painted in the same company livery. I was to learn later that the Ben Line had a financial interest in the berths and godowns in that part of Kowloon. Trust the canny Scots! From the terminal at our destination, which was called Jordan Road, we drove out through even more teeming streets until eventually we broke out into more open and less urban areas. We followed the coast road west with the sea appearing on our left. It was called Castle Peak Road. Some considerable time later we turned sharp right and started to go uphill. In fact very uphill for a very long way. This was a mountain and its name was Tai Mo Shan, the tallest peak in the whole of the Colony. At some point we stopped to take in the view and Mike's dad Bob pointed out some places to me. In the distance through the heat haze you could make out a runway with a small plane about to land on it. I later discovered it was part of the Army complex at Sek Kong and was little used as the runway was short. About ten miles distant to the north was the border with Communist China. It was my first ever view of the Middle Kingdom. Ahead of us at the top of Tai Mo Shan were radio masts and other paraphernalia associated with listening and communications. Bob was full of advice and interesting comments.

'Some of our Boys work up here. Most of them live in Kowloon though with their families and work a funny shift system. Rather them than me I can tell you.' He pointed roughly towards the border over miles of flat land that looked mostly like paddy fields from this distance.

'And up there we have another D/F station called Kon Wei. You wouldn't catch me working there either. One bloke found a snake in the radio shack the other day.'

Half an hour later and we were swimming in the pool, as promised. It was quite surreal to me to find myself in stifling heat with a three thousand foot mountain two miles to the east and the biggest, and potentially nastiest, communist country in the world about six miles to the north. I don't know how many British troops were garrisoned at Sek Kong but within a year almost every soul in Hong Kong, about four million people, would be mighty thankful they were there.

Finally our car did arrive and a note left at the hotel reception from the Ford handling agents, Wallace Harpers, informed Dad it was ready to collect from their garage on

Lockhart Road which was on the main tram line going into Central District about a mile or so away. Dad asked me if I would go with him to collect it, I suspect because I had a better sense of direction than him. We decided to get there by taxi. A wise move as we would be sure to get there then as Harper's letterhead was also printed in Chinese. We were soon there and after signing all the necessary paperwork we got in with me in the passenger seat in the front. I could sense his uneasiness and it was after all his first drive of a new car and his first ever Ford. He had always been loyal to Morris in the past but the seamen's strike meant he had to cancel the Oxford and the only car immediately available for export following the strike was a Dagenham built Ford Cortina Mk I. He was furious at the time but needs must, as they say. The car was a looker though as Dad did have to admit. It was pale green with a white roof (the only colour available believe it or not) and with a bit of imagination you could dream of a Lotus Cortina. The model, a '1500 Super' was only available for export and for the purists it featured a twin-choke Webber carburettor which gave it a lot more whooomph, as they say.

Things did not start well, literally. Dad flooded the carburettor by accident having depressed the accelerator twice before turning the ignition key. A Chinese mechanic came to the rescue and in pigeon English pointed to the accelerator and said 'no touchy first time no goot' or something like that. This was all too much for Dad who then lit up the first of many Rothmans to be smoked in his new car. Eventually it started and we were off. The journey started badly with a sharp turn left across a tram line. Moss had warned him about trams, to no avail it seems. We eventually got into the correct traffic lane and found ourselves heading towards Central in precisely the wrong direction. Moss had said that if you get lost just head for Victoria Barracks so we did just that. From there I knew where we were and we turned left into Queens Road East. It was all very British! Heading east again I knew we would emerge somewhere near that Sikh Temple. Sure enough ten minutes later we were outside the hotel. I had a horrendous thought.

'Dad, where are we going to leave the car?' I need not have been even remotely concerned. The Lee Gardens Hotel had a large underground car park that was also open to the public and it was possible to purchase a weekly ticket. Panic over.

Several days later it was time to attend the Open Afternoon at school. However the school, St. Georges British Army School, to give it its full title, was not on Hong Kong Island. It was in Kowloon about three miles north of the Star Ferry terminal and not all that far from the airport. We were asked to be there by two 'o' clock so to be on the safe side after lunch at the Sunning House we set off about twelve thirty. This was just as well as you will soon learn. We took a taxi to the Star Ferry a journey of no more than fifteen minutes. So far so good. This was our first trip on the famous green and white ferries all named after stars as you might expect. I always remember the name of the first ferry I went on. It was called Meridian Star. We travelled First Class on the upper deck and the fare was twenty cents. On the lower deck where Second Class was just above the waterline, the fare was only ten cents. A year earlier the company had caused a riot by raising the fare from five cents. For some people it might have been a legitimate grievance but sentiment was whipped up by pro-Communist sympathisers who took advantage of any anti-capitalist thinking to engender support for its cause. It was a foretaste of what was to come the following year in 1967 but eventually agreement on prices was reached.

The Star Ferry Company Ltd. is very famous indeed and can boast a history of operation since 1888. Grandpop had told me a little about it as it was in full swing when he was stationed there from 1910 to 1914. It functioned intermittently in the Second World War as you might expect during the Japanese Occupation but, typhoons apart, its service has been continuous. Many people who have never even been to Hong Kong first heard of the Star Ferry when the actor William Holden disembarked the s.s. *President Wilson*, stepped onto a nearby Star Ferry and met Suzie Wong. The movie *The World of Suzie Wong* grossed over $7m – a lot of money in box office terms in 1960. I digress.

The short ten minute trip across to 'Kowloon Side' took less than ten minutes and I saw in daylight some of the places and features that Squirrel had pointed out to me shortly after our arrival including the Clock Tower just a short walk from the ferry terminal. We disembarked and took a short walk to the taxi rink. It was very hot and the queue was mercifully short. Dad got in the front with Mum, Linda and myself in the back. We felt quite at home. It was a Morris Oxford! Then our problems started when Dad gave him the name of our destination.

'Saint Georges School, Wellington Road, Kowloon Tsai please.' The inscrutable look in the Chinaman's eye did not augur well, I thought.

'You mean KG Five? King Georges School?'

'No, SAINT George not King George.'

'Ah, OK.'

The taxi drove east along Salisbury Road and Chatham Road past the Kowloon Canton Railway terminus then the road veered north. A green park area was on our left and a busy cargo wharf on the right owned by Alfred Holt and

Sons of Liverpool. It was the main berth for the Blue Funnel cargo liners, Ben Line's great rivals on the Far East run. Ten minutes later, and judging by the noise of aircraft nearby somewhere near to the airport, the taxi pulled up outside a school building.

'OK fife dorrar.'

Sadly the large sign by the main entrance read 'King George the Fifth School. Bugger. Telling the driver to wait Dad disappeared inside the building emerging a minute later accompanied by a Chinese chap who probably worked in the school office. He barked instructions to the driver in loud Cantonese. The only bit I understood was 'Waterloo Doe' (Waterloo Road). No wonder the driver had been confused. Dad had got his battles mixed up with his Generals. Ten minutes later we arrived at St. Georges School none the worse for our detour. Just a tad embarrassed. It was just about two 'o' clock. Just as well we set off early.

We walked through the main entrance where a temporary sign directed us into the Assembly Hall where there appeared to be six desks marked First Year, Second Year etc. right up to Sixth Form. There was a member of staff sat at each one. Mum went with Linda to the First Year and I went with Dad to the Third Year. My friend Mike had told me I would be in Class 3A with him. There were no other parents waiting at the desk so we sat down opposite a chap aged in his early sixties, bespectacled and perspiring profusely. He smiled at me and shook hands with Dad.

'George Watson, Deputy Headmaster. How do you do.' He was every inch an Englishman abroad.

Dad reached into his battered briefcase which he had bought in Belgium in 1958. It looked like wartime dispatches had been carried in it, so worn were the straps. He pulled out my last two years reports from Scarborough

Boys High School which he had been asked to bring along in the Joining Instructions. Here we go again. Everything connected to the British Army had 'joining instructions' so on reflection it was a pity they didn't include precise directions to the school itself.

Mr Watson perused my latest report in total silence. I hadn't seen it until the day before. On Dad's instructions the school had posted it to Hong Kong c/o Bob Davis, Mike's dad. It would never have caught up with us otherwise on the *Bendoran*. Watson looked very serious.

'I see Mark has done Latin for a year in Scarborough. Unfortunately Class 3A has been doing it for two years already so he'll be a year behind.'

My spirits rose. Maybe I would be allowed to drop the useless subject. Amo, amas, amat my arse! Watson continued.

'Unfortunately although Mark was in the top set for Maths in Scarborough he will find that he is several months behind Class 3A. I think that Mark is best advised to join Class 3B for the first year and then get promoted to Class 4A in a year's time if he merits advancement.

Wrong decision. An angry Victor Harland blew his top, lit a fag, and aimed a broadside at the hapless Watson.

'Now look here. Mark has turned down a bursary at Scarborough College where he could be a boarder now if he wished. He didn't. He chose to come to Hong Kong and this school. Unless he goes straight into the 'A' stream without any delays he will be on a BOAC flight back to London and your name will be on my Union's hit list and at the Army Education Corp's London Office at the MOD within twenty four hours.'

Watson's ghast was flabbered. He was speechless. Maybe nobody had ever spoken to him like that before. I felt almost sorry for him. He quickly changed tack.

'On the other hand we could put him into Class 3A with perhaps some extra tuition in Maths and Latin for the first term to help him catch up.'

Two more Rothmans and a pleasant chat about Malta in the Fifties later (where Watson used to live) and all was well. That wasn't the end of the story though as I was to find out on the first real day at school the following week.

Linda had no such trouble and was destined for Class 1A with a minimum of fuss. Cooling drinks were served in a refectory next door and about three 'o' clock we were all invited to go back into the Assembly Hall where Chinese staff had arranged lots of chairs, theatre style facing the stage. There was a table with three plain chairs behind waiting for occupants to arrive no doubt. We didn't have long to wait. Mr Watson arrived accompanied by a smart lady aged around fifty. She had short, dark curly hair and introduced herself as the Senior Mistress, Miss Gilbert. She looked a bit like Cleo Lane with short hair I thought. Watson rose from his chair.

'May I introduce Mr Peter Croft, our Headmaster. Please be upstanding.'

Bloody hell. Here we go again. Bloody Army. All ranks and bollox.

Peter Croft, or to do credit to him, PA Croft MA (Cantab) looked very smart indeed. He spoke for around ten minutes. He welcomed us all to Hong Kong and to St. Georges School in particular. He spoke about how the local Chinese population really valued education, despite widespread poverty.

'Look how smart all local kids dress on their way to and from school. This is the only British Forces secondary school in the Colony and I want us to set an example to them, not the other way round. Any pupil who persistently misbehaves will be expelled which will almost certainly result in his or her family's repatriation to UK. That will be their problem not mine. Cigarettes are banned even for Sixth formers.'

I looked down at the ash tray that Dad had purloined from somewhere. Already there were three dog ends in it. I decided this was going to be an interesting, if disciplined, three years. I was not wrong.

CHAPTER 3

The next few days just flew by as we prepared to attend our new school. More 'joining instructions' had arrived about our transport arrangements for getting to school. We were informed that arrangements had been made for Linda and I to use the Royal Navy bus that picked up all the kids from Harcourt Place less than half a mile away on the way to Happy Valley racecourse. Harcourt Place, presumably named after Admiral Harcourt, was where most naval families were quartered as they say in service parlance. An odd word really when you consider the medieval punishment of being 'hung, drawn and quartered.' One morning I had a dummy run and walked there just to make sure it was where I thought it was. It took about ten minutes if that and I was amazed by how many shoe shops I walked past – about eight consecutive shops I seem to remember. There was more greenery in the shape of the Craigengower Cricket Club over on the right with perfectly manicured lawn bowls greens on the other side of a tall tennis court like fence separating the Club from the main road. On the left the shops petered out and Harcourt Place was in fact two blocks of nice looking flats each with front facing balconies. The view from the highest flats would have been quite nice with the Hong Kong Football Club and more open greenery not too far away. The school bus left at seven 'o' clock sharp, an unholy hour by English standards but the little recce would ensure we were on time when the first school day arrived. I was happy.

We purchased all sorts of school stuff from the Wing On department store in Hennessy Road. Pencil boxes, pens, pencils of every lead hardness, rubbers, sharpeners and compasses, dividers and set squares for geometry. If I was indeed so far behind in Maths then I would have to 'look sharp' so to speak. I couldn't really believe I would be that far behind. Could I? Only time would tell.

Mum and Dad had taken the decision to wait for No.8 Gordon Terrace to become vacant in early October. This was good news for me as I liked Stanley and we had already made a few further visits there in the Cortina. I had assumed the status of Navigating Officer and was allowed to sit in the front while Dad was still adjusting. Sadly it didn't last long and I was soon demoted to the back seat and the constant flow of cigarette smoke blown towards the rear seats by the ever open front windows. With at least a further six weeks ahead of us in the Sunning House Dad had negotiated a 'family room' with the added advantage of an en-suite bathroom and a TV. The latter was a particular bonus as to kill time in the evenings we had already seen *Born Free* (twice), *The Liquidator* (twice), *Thunderball* (twice) and *Never So Few* starring Frank Sinatra and Gina Lollobrigida all at the Lee cinema. That made a total of three viewings of Thunderball as we had seen it on board *Bendoran* about half-way down the Red Sea. I swore that the shipboard version was slightly raunchier than that shown in Hong Kong where censors had probably snipped a bit of the scene out where Bond had his evil way in a shower with one of his many conquests. I can remember some of the crew shouting 'go on, James, give her one for me.' I forget who the actress was now.

The TV in our family room was a real boon. There were two channels to choose from called Jade and Pearl both supplied by the Rediffusion Company, the same firm that had supplied TV in Malta a few years earlier. However in practice there was only one channel for us, Pearl, as Jade was all in Chinese. It was lame entertainment though to be honest with some of the same programmes we had seen in Malta with many inane American shows like 'Leave it to Beaver' and 'My Favourite Martian' but for adults '77 Sunset Strip' was still going strong. That marque must have made a fortune for its owners. I have to say though that The News at 6pm daily was excellent as was the first class weather report that always followed.

Two major news items though in those weeks at Sunning House were truly shocking and they were both from the UK. The first report came from the Essex seaside town of Southend. The legendary Big Dipper fairground ride at the Kursaal had collapsed killing two people. We were horrified as only some six weeks earlier we had been to Southend a couple of days before boarding *Bendoran*. We had all ridden on the Big Dipper which was terrifying at the time and we were all close to tears as we watched the report. It could have been us. The second and monumental catastrophe happened in Aberfan, South Wales when a coal slag-heap collapsed and caused a landslide that buried over a hundred innocent children in a school. The tragedy too is that if you ask anyone to recall a memorable news event from 1966 they would probably recall England's World Cup Victory before that disaster. It is probably humankind's way of blocking out bad news rather than a considered thought process.

I mentioned the weather reports. To my mind they were just marvellous. In contrast to BBC weather charts with stick on symbols for rain, cloud, sun etc. overlain onto a child-like map of the UK the Hong Kong Weather Report was a geography lesson in its own right. For starters you got a map of the Far East from Singapore in the south to Japan in the north with the pressure pattern for the whole region. This was particularly important for the Colony as any areas of low pressure either in the South China Sea or the Western Pacific in the summer time could lead to a Tropical Storm developing and then possibly maturing into a full blown Typhoon. How exciting! The Report always started off with the presenter, always a female and often either Chinese or Eurasian, giving you the noon day temperatures for the major Asian cities the previous day. Thus:

'So let's see how our Asian neighbours faired yesterday. Singapore 31 degrees Celsius, Kuala Lumpur 32, Djakarta 34' er what? Celsius?! You have to be kidding. Celsius, or Centigrade, was only for the science labs at school. Or was it? This took me aback I have to admit.

The young lady would plough her way through all the Asian capitals and then followed it up with a general forecast for each city. Thus:

'Singapore will see afternoon rain, Manila will be cloudy with winds strengthening from the north- east, Tokyo will have early morning 'Miss' followed by a very hot day and....'

I think Hong Kongers listened to the forecast for Manila with always slightly more than a passing interest. Any typhoons forming in the South China Sea invariably hit the Philippines first before heading north. That wasn't always the case though. Some of the bigger ones were Pacific storms that covered a vast area and they were constantly monitored by US Navy weather planes operating out of the island of Guam. We were never short of information if ever a storm threatened the Colony and the Royal Hong Kong Observatory was a first class organisation. With its own information from weather balloons, ships at sea and the added assistance of Uncle Sam's Navy they provided a service that was second to none. A school trip to the Observatory two years later was very interesting.

Apart from TV, Radio Hong Kong gave out excellent weather bulletins which whenever a typhoon was within four hundred nautical miles of the Colony were treated with the utmost importance. An example might have sounded thus:

'At 6pm Typhoon Mary was centred three hundred and eighty nautical miles east south east of Hong Kong in the Balintang Channel north of Luzon and is forecast to move west at fifteen knots into the South China Sea. Storm signal number One has been hoisted. A further bulletin will be issued at midnight.'

These storm signals were unique to Hong Kong and intended primarily to give warning to fishermen and the owners of small craft. Signal Number One was purely precautionary and gave notice that a tropical storm was within four hundred nautical miles and might affect the Colony. The term 'hoisted' might seem outdated and rather quaint but you have to remember that in the Sixties very few fishermen would have FM radios aboard their junks and sampans. A metal signal about two metres tall was therefore hoisted like a flag on huge latticed steel pylons close to all areas where they could be seen by the fishing community. I think the Number One Signal was a black triangle from memory. Within hours hundreds of small vessels would scurry into the typhoon shelters at various points around the whole Territory. Squirrel had pointed out the huge Yau

Ma Tei shelter on Kowloon side shortly after we arrived. Now I understood its purpose. Another big one was at Aberdeen on the south side of the Island where at the time thousands of people lived on boats.

Things got a lot more serious when Signal Number Three was hoisted as this indicated constant wind speeds in excess of twenty knots. Numbers Five, Six and Seven indicated even stronger winds with from a specific direction. Eight, Nine and Ten were.....well you'd just better look out, that's all I can say. We only saw a Number Ten hoisted once in our three year stay but I will tell you about that later.

So I very quickly had to adapt to degrees Celsius, wind speed in knots and typhoons measured as being so many nautical miles away, the latter two thanks to US Navy planes no doubt. It is rather odd then that today the US is the only country in the world that still uses Fahrenheit.

The TV weather report was always sponsored, at that time by JAL – Japan Air Lines – with the curled up wings of a red headed crane as its logo on the tail-planes of its Douglas DC8 airliners. Not that we could see the red colour as TV was still black and white in 1966. But JAL was well known in Hong Kong and was often advertised with bright neon lights. You could sure see the red cranes then.

CHAPTER 4

I was not looking forward to the first proper day at school. Just the journey there was going to be an ordeal. Alarm clocks were set for six to be on the safe side as we didn't want any cock-ups on the first day. The hotel staff were very obliging and tea and toast with English marmalade was brought to our room. I remember little curled up rolls of butter floating on cubes of ice to stop them melting. By six forty-five Linda and I headed out for Harcourt Place. It was only just light but already it was hot and humid. By the time we reached Harcourt Place I resembled a ball of puss. And we had another six weeks of this lark. The navy blue Bedford bus emblazoned down the side with large letters in white 'RN' was already parked outside with about a dozen kids aboard ranging from about eleven to sixteen years old. I just thought I would check with the driver first.

'Bus to Star Ferry for Saint Georges School?'

Before he could answer some cheeky kid about twelve bawled out 'You're not Navy so you can't use this bus.'

I gave him a good Yorkshire gobfull in return but this little twat repeated this every day for a week. By the Friday I was totally sick of him so I stuck him one in the ribs. Later I learnt that he was in the B stream and not the sharpest tool in the box. Lower deck material – as my father might have said.

Anyway to continue. The bus left bang on time and turned right down Sports Road past the HK Football Club and picked up the main road into Central that had circumnavigated the racecourse. It was a good short-cut and one that track dependent trams could not of course take. The bus headed into the busy district of Wan Chai and headed west. Within ten minutes or so we were on a road running parallel to the high wall that protected HMS Tamar, the naval base. However we soon hit severe traffic congestion and a multitude of heavy vehicles, cranes and the like announced that a new flyover was being built. It was actually an elevated road which when completed would be higher than the wall and allow you to look down into the basin itself. I found this most entertaining in the years ahead as I will later explain.

At about seven twenty we arrived at Star Ferry and joined a long queue of people lining up to pay the 20 cent fare for the crossing to Kowloon. There were newspaper vendors everywhere and I bought a HK Standard for another twenty cents. All the kids travelled First Class. This was accessed via steps to the upper level of the pier which stuck out about a hundred yards into the harbour. Even at this early hour there were hundreds of folk waiting to board the next available ferry and iron gates controlled the foot flow of passengers to avoid overcrowding I guess. The gates were always slammed noisily by uniformed Star Ferry crew who looked like Chinese versions of Popeye to me. Eventually the gates opened and a flood of humanity cascaded down a steepish ramp that was adjustable for the tides. You then turned sharply onto another smaller ramp that had been lowered from the ferry itself and walked on board. You then either turned left or right, which didn't matter because the ferries were all double ended and were identical fore and aft.

All the seats were reversible so you could either travel facing the direction of travel or not. Your choice.

This was only our second trip on Star Ferry, the first being to the school Opening Day. I felt quite the veteran as I looked around the harbour scene before my eyes. Ship spotting had been an interest since living near Sliema Creek in Malta and this was a nautical paradise as I was to discover over the next three years.

Ten minutes later and we arrived at the Kowloon Terminal adjacent to the huge Ocean Terminal. I joined the crocodile of kids expecting the bus to take us to school to be near to the taxis. Wrong! It was about a five hundred yard walk to Haiphong Road where a line of Army buses awaited us. We got on the nearest one and waited. There was no official departure time. As soon as a bus was full the driver started the engine and set off. All the drivers were British Army Ghurkhas about whom I was to learn a lot in the coming months. It was a short but interesting journey of about fifteen minutes. I recognised Holt's Wharf on the right at which was tied up a black and white cargo liner with a blue funnel, hence the name of the shipping line. On the left we passed the park I had seen on our first trip to school but I was mesmerised by what seemed like dozens of people posing like statues or moving slowly like sloths. I didn't know it at the time but they were all advocates of Tai Chi, an ancient Chinese art of bodily self improvement. A shop called the 'Siberian Fur Store' caught my eye. It seemed a ludicrous location to me for such a business in stinking hot and humid Hong Kong.

The route took us past Boundary Street which had marked the old border with China before the New Territories had been added to the Colony's land mass. Turning north into Waterloo Road (not Wellington) we arrived outside St.

George's School and piled off the bus. I glanced at my trusty Roamer watch which Dad had bought me for my ninth birthday in Malta. It still wasn't even eight 'o' clock. And I had to do this every school day for the next three years? Somebody was having a larf!

Within a few minutes I was escorted to my Class (3A) to meet the Form teacher, a Mr John Kotch. He was dressed all in white – shirt, shorts, long socks and highly polished black shoes. He was polite but firm as I stood alongside his desk. He had a register in front of him that recorded pupils' names as well as Religion (God knows why) and one's father's Force/Rank/Unit/Regiment etc. It was very Army oriented as you might expect. He went through a routine which went well at first until I obviously annoyed him.

'Name?'

'Mark.'

'I mean surname.'

'Harland.'

'First names.'

'Mark Vernon.'

'Religion?'

'C of E.'

'Service?'

'Sorry?'

'Service. Army? Navy?'

'No, my Dad's a civilian.'

'What?' Where?'

'Little Sai Wan.'

'Little Sai Wan what?'

'Sir?'

'Yes, that's right. Little Sai Wan, Sir!'

'You address me as Sir in future please, Harland.'

'Yes...Sir.'

'Where have you come from, Harland?'

'Scarborough. Sir. Yorkshire, Sir.'

'I know where it is. Sit down, Harland. There's a spare seat next to Davis. I understand you were at school together in Malta?'

'Yes, we were...Sir!'

It was relief to sit down, I can tell you. Mike whispered into my ear.

'He does this to all new boys.'

I couldn't wait to see some other poor sod get the same treatment, if only for a laugh. I didn't have long to wait. Within a few minutes there was a loud knock at the door. Another 'new boy' entered all sunburnt and freckled. I did a double take. It was a former fellow class mate from Malta and Scarborough. His name was Adrian Olsen. My heart sank. I had forgotten he was arriving in Hong Kong too. I say sank because three years earlier in a dusty school playground at St. Andrews Army School in Malta, Adrian's antics had resulted in my getting caned for the first and only time. He had brought a toy crossbow to school and we tried to re-enact William Tell's trick of shooting an apple on someone's head. Adrian was the target and I was Tell. I missed hopelessly and the offending arrow with a rubber sucker on the end landed in a teacher's cup of coffee that he was holding at the time. I was still holding the crossbow. Talk about a smoking gun. Anyway, this was going to be fun.

'Name?'

'Adrian.'

'I mean surname.'

'Olsen.'

And so on, until Kotch reached the Sir bit and I found it difficult to suppress a laugh. The class thought it was funny when we reached the 'Scarborough bit.' But not as funny as when the third new entrant, a girl, went through almost the same routine ten minutes later. She was tall and had lovely, long red hair. Her name was Sandra Coupland and she came from.....Scarborough! I had never seen or heard of her before then and it transpired that her father had worked with mine for years. Sandra was not put through the 'Sir' ordeal. I could tell already that Kotch was soft on girls and tough on boys. And so it was to prove over the next two years. Mike was right about the skirt. There were indeed some pretty fillies in the class. The cricket could wait. It would have to, as I was soon to discover.

That afternoon all the new kids were asked to go to the Assembly Hall to receive a talk from the Medical Officer, the 'MO.' Nearly everything connected to the Army was abbreviated or acronymed which was very irritating to newcomers. About thirty of us were all stood up in rows as there were no seats. The 'MO' arrived in khaki uniform and with a hat and a swagger stick looked quite absurd, almost like a character from 'It ain't half hot Mum.' He rattled on for ages about the various dangers that we might be subjected to in the Far East-sunburn, heat stroke, dehydration, mosquitoes, malaria, jelly fish stings, snake bites, shark attacks and then wound his speech up with something like this:

'And finally I want to talk to you about the water. The water here is abominable. It is totally unfit to drink and must first be boiled. Do you understand? Boiled. If you do not boil the water you might catch cholera. If you catch cholera the bottom will not drop out of your world, the world will drop out of your bottom. That's all. Dismiss!'

By the end of the first week I had settled in nicely, well up to a point anyway. I had met all the teachers bar one or two. The school functioned on a six day timetable classified by letters. Thus Monday was A Day, Tuesday B Day and so on. F Day would not occur until the following Monday when the cycle would start again. Latin had started badly for me, Adrian and Sandra as all three of us were a year behind. Thus instead of dropping the useless, dreadful language as I had hoped instead we were given extra homework. Ugh! Invariably Adrian and I would agree to do half of it each and then copy each other's work on the Star Ferry in the morning. Looking back this was not a smart thing to do as we would also copy each other's errors which soon got picked up by the teacher whose name I forget, so minimal was the effect he had on me. Things would improve no end the following year but that was a long time away. In the meantime we just soldiered on with endless declensions, conjugations and battle stories from 'Caesar in Gaul' translated from Latin to English and vice-versa. It was all so pointless. Inside the fly cover of one of my textbooks that looked as if it had been in Hong Kong since before the Japanese Occupation some wag had written in stylish copperplate writing:

'Latin is a language As dead as dead can be It killed the Roman Empire And its fxxxxxx killing me!'

It was hard to believe that two thousand years after Rome had conquered Britannia, a colony of the latter six thousand miles away was still learning the language of the former's Empire that had dissolved one thousand six hundred years ago. You couldn't make it up. Caesar must be laughing his nuts off somewhere in the starry firmament. If indeed he made it there. Mind you at least we were doing our homework on a Star ferry.

Things were fairing much better in the field of mathematics. Yes, we three from Scarborough were behind our contemporaries but Mr Kotch, sorry Sir, was very keen to ensure that we caught up. He said it would take us a term to do so. He was about right.

'What do you know about Trigonometry, Harland?'

'Trigger what, Sir?'

'Oh dear me. Right we'll start at the very beginning. I want you to remember three three-word lines off by heart. They are the whole basis of trigonometry. After that it's easy.'

He wrote them on the blackboard:

Two Old Aunts
Sitting On Horses
Catching A Husband.

Kotch made us repeat it out loud several times like a sort of propaganda mantra. What the heck was all this? We would soon find out.

The other teachers were a mixed bunch, to say the least. As a general rule they were all much younger than teachers in UK. Perhaps the chance of overseas postings with the Army Education Corps attracted younger professionals with a sense of adventure. Most had good degrees in the subjects they were teaching but curiously some of the better ones, and I include Kotch amongst them, had only a MEC, a basic teaching certificate. Quite a number of them were Scots which was unsurprising when you think about it. Scotland had sent her youngsters to every corner of the British Empire whether as teachers, doctors, engineers or soldiers. Perhaps it was to get away from the cold, dark six month winter that pervades north of Emperor Hadrian's Wall. There's a reason for everything.

A case in point was my new French teacher, a Miss McDade, an attractive thirty something from Glasgow. Looking back she was quite 'fit' and always smart. However unfortunately for her she had no sense of smell and was always dripping with perfume. She must have spent a fortune on the stuff but at least it was cheaper in duty free Hong Kong. It was quite a novelty listening to French being spoken in broad Glaswegian. The French teacher I had left behind in Scarborough was a Mr Twelves so quite naturally we all called him 'Douze' but there was no translation for McDade.

Another teacher in Class 3A who made a great impression on me was the Geography master, a Mr Trevor Uff. He often signed memos off as TUff which made me laugh. He had a sense of humour too. He was a Londoner, supported Fulham FC (where he came from) and was also a keen cricketer. In fact he was the wicket keeper for the St. Georges School team. The biggest disappointment for me arriving at St. Georges was to discover that the school did not have its own cricket pitch. I was terribly upset. Back in Yorkshire I bowled for the school in the Under 14s and was looking forward effectively to a double season as cricket is played in Hong Kong's winter not summer. Mr Uff took pity on me and asked me if I would like to come along to a match against KGV, an annual needle match it seemed. He also said that they might be a 'player or two short' and that I and another chap in 3A called Gareth Pearce might have to stand in for them. We both jumped at the chance. We lost.

The English teacher was called Mr Elwyn Roberts, probably aged about forty-ish and always very dapper and correct. Welsh by birth I believe but English by nature, Mr Roberts was also an excellent teacher. When the aforementioned George Watson retired back to UK Elwyn Roberts replaced him as Deputy Head. I will write more about Mr Roberts later. In fact much more. I liked him.

The chemistry teacher was a Mr Lawrence. I did not take to him. He was brusque, burly and bearded and chemistry was not my best or favourite subject to put it mildly. The punishment for anyone caught unnecessarily chatting in class was to spend the rest of the lesson stood on your stool. These were quite high as it was in a chemistry lab and for anyone of moderate height there was the imminent danger of being decapitated by the revolving ceiling fan. Health and safety? What in 1966? You're joking mate.

Finally I must make mention of the PE teacher. He was an obnoxious, odious short-arsed Glaswegian called Fergusson. I don't know why but he did not like me from day one. The feeling was mutual. He was a sadist in my book. You will see why later.

CHAPTER 5

Week followed week and very soon we could move from the Sunning House Hotel to our own flat in Gordon Terrace, Stanley. It was a huge relief when the great day arrived. The hotel and staff were just fine but in the end you get sick of the same hotel menus, the endless walks around Wing On's, China Products and Daimaru. Mum was actually looking forward to cooking again and living near to Joyce, her friend of many years. It would be a great adventure for us kids too. There was a whole new world to explore.

In a funny sort of way I was sorry to leave the bus ride to and from Harcourt Place every day. The Navy kids had eventually become quite friendly. Even the B streamer with the sore ribs. He once asked me if I would like to visit his dad's ship when it was due to come on an operational visit. I had taken this as the daydreams of an 'eejit' until I learnt that his surname was Hampshire and that the visiting vessel was *HMS Hampshire* so the lad was either deluded or had a sense of humour. Sadly I was unable to take him up on the kind invitation as I think it coincided with our move to Stanley. I was very disappointed as the *Hampshire* was a brand new state of the art guided missile destroyer. It reminded me of an invitation from a classmate in Malta, Vaughan Gordon, to visit his uncle's cruiser *HMS Lion* when it visited Valletta. Sadly that invitation had fallen through too. I had still not set foot on a British warship but that would be put right soon enough.

The move into Gordon Terrace, which from memory was on a Saturday because I was not at school, was traumatic. All the hired furniture from a company called Dolfra had arrived into the empty flat the day before. The name 'Dolfra' was derived from its owners, a Mr Frank Wilks and his Chinese wife Dolly. She was a very wealthy lady and also owned a hotel called the Ascot House in Happy Valley which many of Dad's colleagues often used as an alternative to the Sunning House. You can forget any ideas of a G-Plan three piece suite, three beds, three wardrobes and a table and four chairs. This was Hong Kong and the finest artisans in woodwork in the world were at your service. All the furniture bar the rattan balcony furniture was made from the highest quality teak, rosewood or camphor-wood. It made the stuff we had left behind in store in England look like tat. A couple of weeks earlier I had gone with Dad to Dolfra's office which was also in Causeway Bay only five minute's walk from the hotel. Frank, a semi-retired Brit aged about fifty, gave Dad a San Mig and me a Coke as we glanced through a catalogue of what furniture was on offer. Frank knew the routine and how much to the last HK Dollar the limit of Dad's generous furniture allowance from the Department. At the end of the three years he gave you the option of buying, for next to nothing, the items you had hired. You then shipped them back to UK, again at Her Majesty's expense.

Thus in addition to the basic stuff of life we hired no less than three highly carved and ornate camphor-wood tea chests, a solid rosewood writing desk, a solid rosewood dining table with six matching chairs and ornate hand-sewn

Chinese cushions to match. By the time we had finished the flat looked like a show room for oriental furniture. At first it felt odd but we soon adapted to it.

Until we lived in Hong Kong I had never heard of a 'lift van.' It is a curious use of words but it is essentially a small shed with a flat roof or a very large reinforced wooden crate. Inside it are numerous other, smaller crates and inside those are packing cases. They are the 'Russian dolls' of the freight forwarding industry. The lift van was literally craned onto a forecourt in front of our block of flats with a Chinese gaffer shouting instructions to the crane operator until it was lowered gingerly onto the correct spot. Once again I heard the epithet 'dew lei lo mo' bawled out several times by the gaffer. What did it mean exactly?

The smaller crates were man-handled by coolies up three flights of stairs to our flat, No. 8A 1st Floor and dragged inside on huge pieces of thick corrugated cardboard so as not to scuff the highly polished parquet flooring that characterised most Hong Kong apartments. I had only been allowed one case for my own personal stuff shipped from home and I dragged it to my own designated bedroom which faced the rear of the flat. Nothing inside it was remotely perishable but still I wanted to check that all was well and I soon prised open the heavily stapled box. All was just as I had packed it almost three months earlier in July. My treasures included a telescope, a cricket bat and ball, some books including a twelve book set of Everyman's Encyclopedia, a world atlas without which I could not contemplate life, a Bible presented to me by a former teacher Miss Shaw, a small framed picture of the Dunkirk veteran *Coronia* in Scarborough Harbour to remind me of home and my old Scout sheath knife. That was about it. Everything else I wanted had been brought to Hong Kong on the *Bendoran*. The rest of the day was spent settling in and finding our feet.

It was strange to wake up the next day to an early morning sun that shone right into the flat from the east which instantly made the flat very hot. The previous occupants had taken the roll-up rattan window blinds with them. How inconsiderate could you get? Our immediate neighbours, the Clayton family, had given us milk, tea and a few basics and had even switched the new fridge- freezer on for us twenty four hours previously. Nobody bought bottled water in those days which seems hard to believe looking back. In fact I don't think it was obtainable at any price. That was something that would have to be addressed very quickly 'lest the world dropped out of our bottom' as the MO had told us earlier.

Dad and I ventured down into the 'Village' as everyone dubbed Stanley Market. There were three general stores to choose from and I had assumed that we would follow Moss & Joyce's choice of Stanley Stores. I was wrong. If, instead of turning right down the hill towards the fruit market, you carried straight on towards the Police Station, there were two more stores called Ah Yick's and the North Point Store. Dad walked straight into the latter as if he had been there a hundred times. A beaming chap came from behind a counter and smiled at Dad a hand out-stretched as he did so.

'You Mister Har Rand? Welcome to Stanley. We give you a good deal and a month's credit, no problem.'

An Australian colleague of Dad's had tipped him off that North Point Stores was in fact the Stanley outpost of a much bigger shop in the North Point area where he lived. They had a superior stock and if they didn't have it 'they could get it' according to the helpful friend who had tipped off the owner that a new customer was coming his way. So, for the next three years the vast bulk of our groceries were ordered from this store with the rest being bought at the NAAFI at Stanley Fort about a mile up the hill.

Leaving the store Dad and I decided to take a wander through the village in a circular path which eventually bring us back to where we had left the Cortina which by now he could start without flooding the carb. We walked back to the Police Station, a monument to colonial architecture if ever there was one. It wasn't a big building but was constructed along military lines with a colonnaded frontage and a large open balcony on the first floor. Rising high above the flat roof was Stanley's typhoon signal apparatus, a steel pylon type structure as high again as the building itself with a horizontal yardarm about two thirds of the way up from which would be hung the signals themselves when a typhoon was forecast. Stanley was built on a narrow north south isthmus with the sea being only a couple of hundred yards away to the east and west. The numerous vessels in either direction would have little difficulty in spotting when danger was imminent. A steep street descended from adjacent the police station almost to sea level and brought us to the main permanent shops. At the bottom on the right hand corner was a shop called Mai Tai Kee. We peeked inside to find a wonderful selection of tools, hardware and the like. Another shop dubbed 'Woolworths' by all who lived in Stanley sold virtually every type of clothes you would ever need and, oddly, electrical equipment. It was a strange combination of retails goods but it was obviously a commercial success. We saw a makeshift bar cum café with a juke box blaring out the latest hits and what looked like off-duty squaddies drinking San Mig beer from the bottles. A gutter ran through the cafe directly under one of the tables. It was not exactly the Rovers Return but hey, this is Hong Kong! Another right turn past the fruit market brought us full circle and we were soon back at the Cortina. Fords being fairly devoid of ornaments there was nobody trying to prise anything off the bonnet and we were soon home. The groceries had already been delivered. How about that?

We had our first home made meal (of bacon and beans on toast) washed down with Lipton's tea for three months. It was delicious. So ended our first full day in Stanley and we had hardly started to explore it yet. Tomorrow was another day and the first journey on a new school bus was about to be experienced.

Alarms were set once again for six 'o' clock. I think it was still dark when I first rose. The Army bus left the Shell garage at 06:45 sharp. Imagine that in the UK. The pupils would go on strike but this was school, British Army style. At least thirty kids got on the bus and there was an 'orderly' in the shape of a Welsh lady who was probably the wife of a serving Welch Battalion officer. The driver was Chinese but dressed in Army khaki and was no doubt from locally recruited Auxiliary Forces. I had half expected a sunburnt squaddie to be driving but this was Hong Kong not Malta. The journey followed the now well-worn route up hill, down hill, past Repulse Bay, Deep Water Bay and then the long climb to the top where the new Girl Guide's HQ was under construction. As we started to go downhill again towards the city and the harbour I looked down towards the Happy Valley Racecourse and couldn't believe what I saw. Horses on the roofs of tall buildings being being walked round in circles in the early morning cooler air. So Moss hadn't being pulling my leg after all! At the bottom of Stubbs Road we turned left by the Sikh temple and followed the same route to the Star Ferry as we had done on the Royal Navy bus when living at the Sunning House. Travelling down Stubbs Road gave you a brief glimpse into the temple grounds and quite a good view of the edifice itself. It wasn't exactly the Golden Temple at Amritsar in the Punjab homeland of all Sikhs, but it gave you an inkling of how well travelled the Sikh community was and how it had served in the defence of the British Empire. I soon discovered that Sikhs were employed in many fields of Hong Kong Government as well as private enterprise. As a throwback to their military background many were employed by banks and jewellery stores in a security role and it was not uncommon to see a colourfully turbaned Sikh outside a bank brandishing a shotgun or blunderbuss.

Quite a few school buses seemed to arrive at the ferry at the same time there maybe being about eight separate routes. My friend Mike's bus started half way up the Peak in an area called Mid-Levels which is an odd name for a place if you ask me. What was even stranger was that the block of flats where Mike lived was called 'Mirror Marina' and being half way up a two thousand foot high mountain was nowhere near the sea or a Marina. Once again the ten minute crossing to Kowloon proved useful for Adrian and I to catch up on the extra Latin homework but I had a feeling that somehow we would never catch up the missing year and that the exercise would be totally futile in the long run. Time would prove me right. I did get a great view of the newly arrived HMS *Hampshire* which was berthed alongside of the north arm of HMS Tamar's harbour. She looked absolutely magnificent and was one of a class of eight identical ships that were, in my opinion, the most beautiful ever designed and built for the Royal Navy.

A few more weeks went by and although it was still hot by UK standards 'half-term' arrived and with it a change into school winter uniform. They must be joking it was still around 25C, around 80F in old money and I was still hot and flustered to put it mildly, especially on days when sports was on the timetable. In those days St. Georges did not have its own swimming pool and so this required a bus journey (yet another one) to either the Gun Club Army barracks or, more usually for the boys, to RAF Kai Tak which was only a mile away and immediately adjacent to the civilian airport. I absolutely hated it. I had not been a regular swimmer since we lived in Malta three years earlier and having not long been back in a hot climate I was still untanned and sunburnt. A squadron of RAF Gloster Javelin jet fighters were usually parked only a hundred yards or so from the pool with the tail-planes and engines facing towards the pool. Thus whenever the engines were started for whatever reason a fine spray of aviation fuel would flow like a mist and end up on the surface of the pool rather like petrol or diesel in a puddle of water. It made me feel quite sick but our sadistic Glaswegian, Fergusson, still barked orders from the poolside like some sort of demented Olympic coach blowing his whistle as if he was training a dolphin to leap through a hoop. Something else that did not endear me to this clown was the fact that he kept calling me Sheehy not Harland as he always confused me with another redhead chap who as it happened also lived in Stanley. Unfortunately Sheehy had a permanent reputation in the school for bad and disruptive behaviour and I was thus the butt of many accusations for misdemeanour's of which I had no knowledge. Thus the cry of 'Sheehy, come here boy!' was repeated many times. Even though Fergusson realised he had made an error he never apologised once. I did once get one over on him though as you will see.

An another occasion on a particularly hot afternoon he sent us all on a cross country run the intended route for which took us over the main Kowloon Canton Railway and through an area of quite dense vegetation. I soon fell behind the rest. Fergusson had told us to beware of oncoming trains and to take care when crossing the line. You can forget any idea of the York to Kings Cross express doing about eighty knots. Most of these trains managed about a quarter of that, especially the heavily laden goods trains. I heard one coming and decided to wait for it to pass. It took for ever and to my surprise every single goods carriage was full of live pigs. Sweet and sour pork never seemed quite the same after that. I had lost my bearings by now and I was very hot and very thirsty. I retraced the route I thought I had come on previously from the school and was shocked to see a snake about three feet long slither into the grass from the rough path I was walking along. I don't like snakes and this caused an increase in speed from two knots to about six. When I eventually got back to the school Fergusson was furious with me.

'Where the fxxx have you been, Sheehy?' I told him I had been delayed by a train, got lost and had seen a snake on the route. 'Rubbish, Sheehy' was all he said.

About a week later the Headmaster, Mr Croft, made an announcement during morning assembly that a young Chinese boy had been bitten and seriously injured by a snake near the railway line and that the area was now 'Out of Bounds' for all pupils. I was sorry for the boy but I must confess I had a good chuckle to myself. Cross country running was soon replaced by another totally pointless so called sport called Orienteering. Mind you at least we were in the right part of the world!

The absence of a school cricket pitch was a colossal disappointment. In fact the school had only one sports field which was used for football, hockey and field sports like discuss and javelin. I had a good throwing arm being a bit of a bowler and I was as good as the next at the javelin which I could sense annoyed Fergusson. If only he could have been the target I might have improved even more. On the plus side Hong Kong's winters are bone dry and thus the sports field was far too hard for rugby, a game I detested and had been forced to play back at the grammar school in Scarborough.

The genial Mr Uff though had arranged for Gareth Pearce and myself to make use of the HK Cricket Club's facilities at Chater Road on the Island side only five minutes walk from the Star Ferry. So after school every Friday Gareth and I walked there and used the Club's nets for at least an hour or so to keep our eye in. I usually bowled with Gareth preferring to bat. There was a very active cricket club league in Hong Kong and competition was fierce. Where Dad worked, Little Sai Wan, even had its own team and their ground was the envy of every other Club as I will explain later. After practising at Chater Road we would either get the Number 6 bus home or Gareth's dad would pick us up in his Singer Chamois which was a very trendy car in those days. The Pearce family lived at Repulse Bay on the way to Stanley and when given a lift I would hop out and take the bus the last three miles or so. Within a year photographs of the HK Cricket Club would be on the front page of newspapers all over the world for all the wrong reasons.

CHAPTER 6

The summer of '66 turned to Autumn, perhaps the nicest time of year to be living in Hong Kong. The temperatures dipped down to around 20C and the dreaded humidity lowered to acceptable levels. Navy blue blazers were the order of the day for school uniform and we all had to wear ties, even the girls. The school had a 'House system' for all competitive events. At my previous Army school, St Andrews in Malta, the Houses were named after famous WW2 Generals and Field Marshals and I half-expected the same sort of thing in Hong Kong. In the event they were named after the Royal Houses of Britain, namely Balmoral, Windsor and Sandringham depicted by the colours yellow, red and blue respectively. Thus if you were in Balmoral House, like me, your school tie had a yellow weave to it and so on. There was great competition to see who could tie the craziest knots in their ties, the Windsor knot being favourite as you might imagine. With the donning of long winter trousers for the winter months gone were the long white socks with garters where Sixth formers secreted a few fags to smoke on the ferry or before you got on the Army bus for the final leg home.

The more acceptable weather also meant that we were more adventurous in the car at weekends. We extended our range of outings in the Cortina and we could now drive clockwise around the whole of Hong Kong island, a distance of over twenty five road miles, without getting too lost. The drive to Little Sai Wan, which Dad did every day to work, was quite an adventure and entailed a journey of about seven miles going anti-clockwise from Stanley via Tai Tam reservoir which was only made a reservoir when a large dam was built across the Bay allowing the numerous summer season rains to fill it. The main road was actually along the top of the dam itself but its narrow width allowed for the passage of vehicles one way at a time with traffic lights to control the flow. This was also the main bus route from Stanley to Shau Ki Wan at the eastern end of the main urbanised city area. After crossing the dam the road climbed steeply for about two miles and brought you to a crossroads, left to the city or right to Shek O and Big Wave Bay, two favourite beaches in the summer months. This was also the only route, by road at least, to Little Sai Wan and the first time Dad took the family there one weekend was a revelation to say the least. The place had the air and atmosphere of a 'Country Club' not a highly secretive listening base. It was extensive and covered about a hundred acres. The main 'office' buildings were of mostly two storeys and painted white and surrounded by tall masts and radio ariels which obviously represented the business end of the operations. Behind them the land rose sharply forming a natural layer of physical protection. In front facing the sea and the narrow Lei Yue Mun Channel it was a different matter. Much land reclamation had taken place giving rise to a football pitch, a cricket pitch, tennis courts and, believe it or not, a Yacht Club! In addition there were small houses for the locally employed staff with some of them keeping pigs in enclosed gardens around them. Families used 'Sai Wan' for recreation at weekends and kids who spent the weekdays in school and apartment blocks, particularly those who lived in urban areas like Mid-Levels, could let rip and enjoy the fresh air and sports facilities. A building called 'Ariel House' had a restaurant, bar, snooker room and with its long open balconies afforded great views of the cricket matches that took place most weekends in the winter months. The contrast with my home town's cricket ground at North Marine Road in Scarborough could not have been greater. In the Sixties possibly up to half of the men who worked at Sai Wan were Australians, mostly serving RAAF members normally based either in Perth, Western Australia or Melbourne, Victoria. For most of them this was there first time leaving Australia. As you might expect many of them were keen cricketers and there was never any shortage of volunteers to mow and roll the pitch. It was hallowed ground to some of the Diggers and the following year the visiting Defence Secretary, Denis Healey, created an almighty row when the Army helicopter in which he was being taken to Little Sai Wan inadvertently landed on a newly prepared wicket. Living in Stanley as we did where open air and beaches were freely available we did not use Sai Wan as much as many families but it was always there for an occasional weekend jaunt and was a nice change for Mum and Joyce who delighted in having a Sunday lunch put in front of them for a change. Not that roast beef and Yorkshire puddings were ever available but the range of Oriental dishes laid on by the locally employed cooks was just amazing. You never actually paid cash for anything either. Dad was given a Bar No. and you simply signed a chit, added the Bar No. and Bob's your Uncle. It was unreal.

As Sai Wan Bay was at the eastern approaches to Hong Kong harbour all manner of shipping was easily observable and every type of vessel from many different nations could be seen on any day, many recognisable from their company livery or if not then from the recognition ensign they flew from the stern. Some were so close to shore you could even read their names on the forecastle or if you missed it then the names and ports of registration were visible on the stern as they had to be by international law. Ships from the great trading nation of Japan were regular sights with the suffix 'Maru' an almost compulsory addition to their nomenclature. Maru means circle in Japanese implying that ship went full circle and always came 'home' to Japan. Mitsui OSK Lines was probably the most familiar Japanese company. British lines included the Ben Line with which we were of course very familiar having arrived ourselves on the *Bendoran* and the blue grey hulls, white superstructures and yellow buff funnels were spotted frequently. The competing Blue Funnel Lines were highly visible too and all seemed to have Greek names like Cyclops, Socrates and the like.

It wasn't just ship spotters like me that enjoyed the vista from Sai Wan. Aircraft approaching Kai Tak Airport from the south-east made their approach directly overhead Sai Wan and in the days when noise regulations were almost non-existent the aero engine manufacturers like Pratt & Whitney concentrated on power not noise abatement. You sure knew when a plane was coming and they passed over at about a thousand feet with their undercarriage already lowered as they clawed their way to the safety of the concrete ribbon of the main runway at Kai Tak probably about four miles distant as the crow, or even the Boeing 707, flies. In the mid-Sixties the most common airlines that flew in and out of Hong Kong were not surprisingly those that belonged to neighbouring Asian countries such as Taiwan, Japan, Malaysia and Singapore although in those days the latter two nations jointly owned an airline called MSA – Malaysia Singapore Airlines. When the two countries fell out politically it de-merged into Singapore Airlines and MAS – Malaysian Airline Systems. Other more distantly based airlines however showed up in the skies every day.

St Georges School was only a mile from the airport runway so if the aircraft coming in to land did not make their final approach over Sai Wan then they had to do it over land almost directly over the school itself and at that point in the procedure they were not more than five hundred feet above the ground and probably fifteen to twenty seconds from touchdown. Before the school had air-conditioning installed in late 1968 all the windows were open and ceiling fans recirculated the hot, humid air with an awful lot of noise as a result when a plane flew in. Thought, let alone speech, was impossible for probably about fifteen seconds as the sound-print travelled over you then ceased as the plane hit the deck about a mile to the south-east. A passing Caravelle of Thai International or a Convair Coronado of Cathay Pacific provided many a welcome diversion from a boring History or Latin lesson. Learning about English Roundheads and Cavaliers just didn't seem relevant when you were eight thousand miles away and as for Latin, well you know my thoughts on that already. Two afternoon flight arrivals that you could almost set your clock by were operated by Pan Am and BOAC. The former was a leg of its famous PA1 flight which flew from New York to New York from west to east and geographically Hong Kong was about half way. Flight PA2 flew the same flight in the opposite direction. Pan Am and BOAC were probably the two best airlines in the world at the time but sadly today they no longer exist, one falling victim to financial mismanagement the other to a British Government hell bent on the political dogma of privatisation. Today international aviation is the poorer without them.

Several events stick in the memory for the rest of that Autumn term. With the weather cooling and very pleasant there was a Sports Day at Little Sai Wan, I think in early November. Every son and daughter between five and eighteen was given the opportunity to enter races of their choice whether it was straight running, the 'sack race' or the egg and spoon race. It was a lovely sunny afternoon and hundreds of folks turned up. There were a few outside sponsors in the shape of local companies that exhibited and gave out freebies to both parents and kids. You might find this very hard to believe but one of the sponsors was *555 State Express Tobacco*! There were two or three very pretty Chinese PR girls in attendance bedecked in the yellow and purple sashes that were the hallmark of *555* and they handed out free packets of fags to all the winners! Imagine the 'health police' today if they saw that happening. But that was Hong Kong in 1966 and hey anything goes as long as it oils the wheels of commerce. Cigarette ads were very prevalent on TV and some of them were so banal and simplistic it wasn't true. I remember one from *Winston* that depicted a playboy type dude on the bow of a racing yacht moving at high speed and lighting a fag with a Zippo lighter without his long locks fluttering one iota in the strong breeze. It was obviously a superimposed studio shot.

November the 11th brought Mike's fourteenth birthday and he celebrated by holding an evening Bar B Q at St. Stephen's Beach in Stanley. I think most of our class was there and Mike's dad, Bob, brought most of the food and drink in the capacious boot of his Zodiac. This included quite a few bottles of San Mig beer. I had drunk one or two illicit tins of Harp lager on the *Bendoran* en route to

Hong Kong courtesy of our Irish priest friend Paddy so I considered myself a veteran of course. Sadly within a few minutes of consuming a whole bottle I was sick. I did however manage to perform the 'technicolour yawn' out of sight behind a large rock to avoid embarrassment. It was yet another lesson learned the hard way.

My progress at school was very mixed. The Latin was just awful and there was no way I was ever going to catch up, not that I particularly wanted to. The Latin words for helmets, swords, spears and battles were useless in a land where ninety-nine percent of the people around you spoke Cantonese – the dialect of most of southern China. We had two teachers called Williams, a Mr Williams taught biology and a prissy Miss Williams taught history. As you might expect the biology had a local flavour to it. A large snake skin adorned one of the biology lab walls which was bad enough but somebody caught a live snake about three feet long and it lived in a glass tank for many months. One of my class mates, Gerald Simpson, was a bit of a wag to say the least and he liked to torment the snake by banging on the side of the glass with a ruler until it eventually struck out repeatedly in his direction, only to be stopped by the thick glass thank goodness. Mr William's assertion that it was 'harmless and non venomous' did not allay my own fears and to this day I have reserved a healthy dislike of most reptiles. However I liked biology and Mr Williams was a very nice chap.

Maths, on the other hand, was going very well indeed and by the end of the term I had just about caught up the rest of the class. John Kotch was a superb teacher. I learnt that 'Two old aunts, sitting on horses, catching a husband' was to teach you the basic rules of trigonometry. Thus for all triangles containing a right angle, to which trigonometry always applies, the Tangent equals the Opposite over the Adjacent, the Sign equals the Opposite over the Hypotenuse and finally the Cosign equals the Adjacent over the Hypotenuse. Wow! This will mean nothing to the non-mathematician but believe me back in 1966 it saved my bacon. By the end of the year Mr Kotch wrote in my school report: 'I expect Mark to be ready to sit 'O' level Maths a year earlier than usual.'

One morning immediately after Registration and Assembly, Mr Kotch read out a memorandum from some Army bigwig. It announced that a limited number of places were available for a Driving Course to be conducted on Saturday afternoons. 'Those interested' etc.....you bet!

CHAPTER 7

Three of us from Class 3A put our names forward, Mike, myself and a chap called Cliff Dive. There was only one problem with this new adventure – the location. The Course was to take place at a disused tank range at a place called Dill's Corner in the northern New Territories right up near the border with China. Exactly who 'Dill' was I had no idea. As ever 'joining instructions' arrived from the Army and the best advice was to travel on the Kowloon Canton Railway from the southern terminus near Star ferry to a station called Sheung Shui. The memo went on:

'All civilians are to alight at Sheung Shui without fail as the next station, Lowu, is out of bounds to all non-military and non-HK Police personnel.'

The warning was apposite. The little town of Lowu was just a few hundred yards from the Shum Chun River which officially marked the border between British Hong Kong and Communist China. It wasn't just a geographical border. It was a great military and political divide as well. The rumblings of Mao's Red Guards were getting ominously louder and the crackdown of the Revolutionary Guards against civil unrest was becoming ever more vocal and brutal. Trains didn't actually cross the border despite the tendency to believe otherwise from the title of the train company which was usually abbreviated to the KCR.

From Sheung Shui station the only way to travel to Dill's Corner was by an illegal (at that time) mini-bus taxi service known as a Pak Pie. I don't think this was ever a reference to anything edible and it was simply colloquial Cantonese for an illegal taxi. The fares were fixed at 1HK$ per journey no matter how long or short the distance covered.

So the first Saturday of the driving course duly arrived and we three arranged to meet at the Star ferry on Hong Kong side, probably at about 1pm. Cliff's father, another Bob, joined us as somehow he had been roped in to act as an instructor. Having crossed the harbour we went to the ticket booth. I think it was the first time on the KCR for any of us, even Mr Dive who had been in the Colony two years. Immediately we were faced with a dilemma.

'You wan furs, secon or turd crass?'

We all opted for Second Class. From memory there were only three passenger carriages, one for each Class, pulled by a huge green diesel locomotive that was probably powerful enough to pull five times that number of coaches. My mind flashed back to the 'pig train' I had seen on the aborted cross country run and I smiled. At least there wouldn't be any livestock on this train. Wrong! Our carriage wasn't full by any means but several passengers were carrying wire baskets full of live chickens. I took a look through into 'turd class' and saw that ducks and chickens way outnumbered humans and it was heaving with both. I resolved that next time I would travel 'Furs Crass' as the difference in fares was minimal.

A whistle blew and the train moved slowly out of the station. Within seconds we were passing the grandiose Peninsula Hotel on the left and Holts Wharf on the right. The track soon veered left into a built up area and I lost my bearings. We picked up a little speed and headed roughly north passing closest to St. Georges about ten minutes later although you could not see the school from the train. The train soon sounded its horn and we entered into a long tunnel which was called the Lion Rock Tunnel. In Cantonese the word 'Kowloon' means nine dragons which referred to the nine hills on the roughly triangular peninsula with the bottom of the triangle aiming like a dagger towards the harbour and HK Island. Lion Rock was the tallest and most impressive 'dragon' so called because from certain angles it resembled a lion's head, so they say anyway. We emerged from the tunnel after about thirty seconds into a totally different world. There was greenery and fields everywhere you looked and there was not a building to be seen. Was this the same country? The first stop was a small town called Sha Tin which was sited at the head of a long narrow coastal inlet. You could see paddy fields everywhere and a multitude of small boats in the inlet. Today Sha Tin is the site of a magnificent racecourse to complement Happy Valley but in the Sixties it was just a small stop on the KCR. A few people got off and a few more people (and ducks) got on. The train chugged north north east following the coastal inlet until it stopped again at a place called Tai Po. It was a proper fishing village with a lot more boats visible. How long was this going to take? We were supposed to be at Dill's Corner by 2pm and it was getting on for that already. There were still two more stops to go including Fan Ling, the location of a popular and expanding golf course which today is the home of the Hong Kong Open. On arrival at Sheung Shui there were civilian HK Police officers on hand to ensure that nobody stayed on the train who wasn't entitled to. It was surprisingly easy to acquire a Pak Pie and ten minutes later we arrived at the tank range. And so began my first ever driving lesson in, of all vehicles, a VW Campervan!

I don't know about the others but I was expecting maybe an old Army Land Rover or maybe a beat up old Morris Minor. There were three other normal cars including a Ford Zodiac, a Zephyr Six and something else. By about four 'o' clock the lesson came to an end and I learnt to drive albeit it at about five knots and never moving out of second gear.

In the following weeks we wisely took an earlier train to lengthen the available driving time and within a month or so I was driving the Zephyr solo. Sorry to say that I was responsible for an accident when I drove the front end of the Zodiac directly into a huge pile of water buffalo dung. It was the column gear change that threw me as I struggled to find a gear and coasting at high speed in neutral (probably about fifteen knots) I realised, too late, that a meeting with some deep fried doo dah was inevitable. Somebody must have told Mr Kotch because he pulled my leg several times over the incident. Oh well, 'neffer mine' as they say in China.

On those Saturdays it was almost dark by the time I got back to Stanley. The end of term was in sight and the Christmas Holiday was not too far away. Christmas's in Christian Malta had not been very much different to England but what would they be like in Hong Kong? None of the family had ever had a Christmas in the Tropics apart from Dad in his WW2 navy days.

The Post Office at the NAAFI at Stanley Fort reminded us that there were only so many days left for guaranteed surface Christmas mail to UK so any intended parcels had to be planned well ahead. We decided to send two large parcels, one to Mum's father in Scarborough and another to Dad's Aunty Nell in Edmonton, North London. Aunty Nell would open the parcel and distribute the smaller ones contained inside to other family members including my paternal grandparents. One item though would be common to both parcels – a supply of roll-up tobacco. Dad settled on tins (in those days) of St. Julien tobacco which in the UK was considered to be a superior quality. Six tins were purchased in the NAAFI, two for my grandfather in Scarborough, two for Nell's husband Sydney and the remaining two for Grandpop, also in London. Dad had been tipped off by a colleague that HM Customs in UK were as keen as mustard to charge Excise Duty on all secreted tobacco and even X-rayed parcels from overseas Forces Post in the hunt for extra revenues. The trick, as Dad was told, was to put 'stainless steel ashtrays' in the contents box on the Customs declaration. It worked! For three years umpteen tins of St. Juliens ended up in Scarborough and Edmonton. Also in the parcels were high quality wool jumpers, silk ties, Chinese snuff bottles and other little trinkets that would not be available in England. The wrapping process became almost a ritual with a strong cardboard box containing all the gifts being covered in at least three layers of old fashioned brown paper, each individually sellotaped, thick string criss-crossing all six sides of the ultimate package and if that was not enough, a multitude of large red blobs of sealing wax over every overlap of paper. For good order even the final knot in the string, almost certainly a naval bowline, was entombed in a huge red blob. It was almost as if Dad was waging a personal war with HM Customs.

Whether that was his intention or not I can report that in almost three years not one parcel failed to arrive and not one penny was paid in duty.

Another St. Georges pupil who lived in Gordon Terrace was called Alan Jones who was a year higher than me. What he lacked academically he more than made up for in musical talent. He was a very clever guitarist both Spanish and electric. He started to give me rudimentary lessons at weekends and within a couple of weeks I was able to play such complicated pieces as Ba Ba Blacksheep and Twinkle Twinkle Little Star. I also discovered that if you played the former slowly it actually sounded remarkably similar to the latter. I must confess though that I only discovered this by accident as I could only play it slowly. I did however manage to learn a quite complicated opening piece of a famous flamenco which sounded quite amazing but I was hampered by a total inability to read music. News got back to my father. This was not good because as a surprise Christmas present he bought both my sister Linda and I a Spanish guitar together with a course of twelve lessons from a renowned Spanish and Hawaiian guitar teacher called Raymond Lui. The lessons were to commence in January and to take place after normal school every Tuesday. This was exactly what I didn't want! It immediately brought back memories of a time in Malta over three years earlier when Dad, under false pretences, had steered me into a music shop in Valletta to sign me up to violin lessons with one Professor Vallente. I had ran out the shop in shock horror. And now he was doing it all over again. Weren't the damned school days with all that travelling quite long enough?

As we mutually promised, we kept contact with our new friend Father Patrick Corcoran from the days on *Bendoran* and we visited him at the Salesian School in Shau Ki Wan several times. The school was a miracle of civil engineering built as it was into an almost vertical hillside with umpteen floors and mezzanine levels. There were table tennis courts everywhere you turned and I had never seen so many pupils crammed into a school. What was even more astonishing was that Patrick told us that effectively three schools operated there at the same time – a morning, afternoon and evening school – such was the demand for a top quality education.

True to its Salesian principles the education was free if you could not afford it and many of the boys lived in huts and hillside settlements or cubicles in awful tenement buildings. People living in such parlous conditions were slowly being rehoused in Government sponsored 'Resettlement Estates' where at least the basic necessities of life were provided like clean water, sanitation and a waterproof roof over your head. I will write much more about these estates later. So where did the money come from to finance this amazing school? Patrick explained that the parents of some of the boys were very wealthy indeed and made massive donations. They were never short of money and what you didn't have then the Good Lord will provide. Christmas was not too far way and Paddy asked my Dad if he would kindly play the role of Father Christmas at the school's Christmas Party which was coming up soon. He promised Dad a fun time. How could he refuse? In the event he enjoyed it so much he volunteered to do it for the next three years. It was apparently the first time many of the kids had seen a 'Gweilo' (a foreign devil) as Father Christmas and Patrick said it made the party all the more authentic for that. Quite how the myth of Father Christmas was interwoven with Catholic teachings was left to Paddy.

Christmas and New Year came and went, as they do wherever you are in the world. The weather was warm but not hot and everybody in Gordon Terrace socialised, going into each others flats for drinks and nibbles before one's own roast turkey. There were even frozen sprouts, God forbid. We did all have phones but they only worked within the Colony and no system was yet in place to enable you to phone grandparents back in England. It had been a tradition in Mum's family to cook a brace of pheasants on New Year's Day. They were all farmers and on Boxing Day would go out shooting with 'the bag' being hung in sheds until New Year's Eve when the men would pluck and dress the shot game to prepare it for the feast next day. It was a tradition that we had thought we would be unable to comply with in tropical Hong Kong. We were wrong. Dad's colleague had been right when he said that the North Point Stores 'could get anything for you' and we were amazed to get a call saying that they had sourced several brace for us from a Chinese importer. Perhaps when you consider that the pheasant is an endemically Asian bird that was introduced into Europe by traders in the nineteenth century it is not such a surprise. Anyway several guests were invited to join us for dinner on New Year's Day in the time honoured way.

Toasts were made and 'Auld Lang Syne' was sung but none of us could have predicted what was in store for us in 1967. We were all in for one heck of a shock.

CHAPTER 8

The Peoples Republic of China was in total turmoil. That is putting it mildly. The so called 'Cultural Revolution' was in full swing and although the immediate effects fell on China's booming population it was starting to cause ripples of discontent in the Colony. Anything that caused the slightest bad feeling amongst the local population, such as bus or ferry fare increases, was grabbed on by communist inspired unions and amplified. Did an increase in a bus fare from say twenty to twenty five cents really cause that much hardship? If you were in a well paid profession it didn't but you have to take into account that the vast majority of local workers earned only three hundred Hong Kong dollars per calendar month. That equated to about twenty pounds a month or five pounds a week, about a quarter of the average wage in the UK at the time. For that money you had to work ten hours a day for six days a week and for those who say worked in a sweat shop garment factory life was very hard indeed. Thus it was easy for leftist agitators to stoke up civil disorder. The Hong Kong Government was in a permanent quandary. The Colony was booming and revenues were going through the roof but do you spend that money on housing, infrastructure, education or what? They were not easy days for the Governor, Sir David Trench, to put it mildly. He had overall responsibility for the good governance of Hong Kong and he was the Commander in Chief of all British Forces in the Colony. The burden on his shoulders was awesome and increased in gravity as the weeks and months rolled on. Trench, or to give him his full and correct title, His Excellency the Governor Sir David Trench, was the Queen's representative in the Colony and reported directly to the Foreign Secretary in London. At the time that person was George Brown, the MP for Belper in Derbyshire. I never met him but I know a few people who did. It is one of the great anachronisms of the British political system that one man could be jointly and coincidentally responsible for a small Derbyshire mill-town and a colony of four million people eight thousand miles away.

In early February we experienced our first Chinese, or Lunar, New Year. This was something new for us and indeed all new-comers to Hong Kong. Chinese New Year is celebrated by the second new moon after the winter solstice. Thus it can take place in January or February, depending. This seemed awfully strange but when you compare it to the Christian Easter Sunday which is the first Sunday after the first full moon after the Spring solstice then it makes you wonder if all the ancient religious calendar formulators were drinking the same home brew. Needless to say it was a public holiday. In fact most shops and businesses stayed shut for three days but our friendly suppliers at North Point Stores had tipped us off to make sure we didn't run out of essential provisions like beer and cigarettes. There were an awful lot of fireworks going off seemingly all the time and I was amazed to discover that you could actually buy them all year round if you knew which shops to go to. It was a cause for great celebration amongst the locals and a long brightly coloured dragon carried by a dozen or so young men danced and pranced their merry way around every part of Stanley to the constant accompaniment of noisy fireworks of course. To top it all an ornamental lion arrived at the courtyard in front of Gordon Terrace with a huge drum being constantly beaten to a volume and rhythm that would not have been appreciated by anyone sleeping after a night shift at Little Sai Wan. Young boys ran up the stairs to every flat with a silver dish to collect money for 'fishermen's welfare' and they did well I think. I was under strict instructions to donate a dollar from my pocket money. 'Kung Hei Fat Choi' or Happy New Year was the constant mantra. We were happy to reciprocate and those words were probably the first ones we could pronounce properly. There was another reason why all local Chinese were happy. It was the tradition to be paid double your salary for the month in which the New Year fell. Thus most people were paid thirteen months salary every twelve months. I say most people. There was one exception which I will touch on later.

By about March things were not looking too good and the industrial unrest and street demonstrations augured badly for a long hot summer ahead. How true that proved to be. There were industrial disputes in shipping, transport (including taxis I recall) and a major dispute in the world's biggest factory producing, of all things, artificial plastic flowers. These disturbances were actively encouraged by communist union members and the HK Police made many active arrests, raiding premises on an almost daily basis. The PRC Government in Peking supported the unrest with radio broadcasts and money for the communist leaning leftist newspapers including the Ta Kung Pau which was published in English. Sir David held firm and no doubt took almost daily advice from London.

One of the advantages of going to a Services school was the incredible amount of information gleaned from playground chatter and gossip. Every department of the military was represented by pupils who would say things like:

'Dad says more Hunter jets are arriving from Singapore tomorrow' or 'Dad says an aircraft carrier is being diverted to Hong Kong as a show of strength.'

It was all quite worrying because nobody knew where it would all end. If a million Red Guards decided to invade Hong Kong there would be absolutely nothing either the HK or British Governments could do about it. Years later it transpired that many senior members of the Chinese Politbureau were in favour of invading the Colony but the idea was personally vetoed by the then Premier Chou En Lai. It was a wise move on his part.

At Easter everybody's eyes were taken off the political ball by unseasonable torrential rainfall. We were off school for the Easter Hols of course and I had never seen rain like it before, nor since. The Royal Observatory's warning over Radio Hong Kong was very much to the point:

'A stationary trough of low pressure extends from east to west over southern China and is expected to bring heavy rain for several days. There is a danger of landslides in hilly areas...etc.'

The Observatory wasn't underestimating the seriousness of the situation. On Good Friday we had no less than four inches of rain in one hour. I remember it very well. It was mid-morning and Dad and I were installing a Telefunken music centre into the flat. We ran out of speaker wire and the associated clips to fasten it to the skirting boards. Dad suggested that I walk down to the village to see if I could acquire some from an electrical shop. I looked outside. It was as dark as night and the rain was so heavy you could barely see twenty yards. Not one to decline a challenge I ventured out with folk probably watching from the other seventeen balconies wondering if I had lost my marbles. Unlike cyclonic rainfall associated with strong winds and typhoons this rain was straight up and down so a large umbrella did the trick. I think I was probably the only 'Gweilo' who ventured into the village that day. By lunchtime the radio was giving out reports of roads closed due to landslides. Another thing that sticks in my memory about the radio whenever bad weather came along was the gentility of announcements that were made, seemingly every few minutes by presenters. They would read something like this:

'Owing to the inclement weather, the Sandy Bay Children's Home picnic scheduled for this afternoon at Middle Bay is cancelled.'

Inclement? Four inches of rain in an hour! In was gross British understatement at its finest. Landslides were very bad news indeed particularly if you were a recent refugee living in a hillside hut awaiting resettlement to one of the new estates. People often died. The basic geology of Hong Kong was a problem that no Government and no amount of expenditure could solve. More than ninety percent of HK's rocky outcrops consisted of decomposed red granite which looked like sandstone but geologically was anything but. Anything sedimentary, that is laid down in hard layers, would have stood up much better to the affects of rain and sun but old, igneous, eroded granite would tumble down like sand through an egg timer. Hillsides that were regularly prone to collapsing were often plastered over with great swathes of mortar so that rainwater could rush down unhindered into man made drains and nullahs. I recall that the road between Stanley and town was closed for a couple of days over that Easter while work gangs made repairs to the road. Why couldn't it happen in term time when a couple of days off school would have been much appreciated?

And talking of school things were not going very well academically speaking. Maths and English were fine but with the exception of Geography my grades were in decline on every other subject. Unless I pulled my socks up then demotion to Class 4B the following year was a possibility that my end of term report spelled out in black and white. Dad was furious and Mum was upset. Repatriation to the UK and becoming a boarder at Scarborough College was openly discussed. To be honest I was knackered, mentally and physically. The days were incredibly long starting at six in the morning because of travelling times and to make things worse two hours of bloody homework were superimposed in the evening with even more at weekends. I thought it was a damned cheek to be honest. The Army bigwigs that set the hours worked 'tropical hours' and knocked off at lunchtime. Not for them a long bus ride, a cross harbour ferry followed by a walk and another sodding bus. Similarly all the teachers bar none lived in Kowloon and some even walked to work. I was not happy but on the plus side the guitar lessons had come to an inglorious end. Mr Lui deemed me to be 'musically inept' which I could have told him (and Dad) at the very beginning. Manitas de Plata I was not going to be.

I upset the Chemistry teacher, Mr Lawrence, one day and not for the first time either. He was a totally humourless man. The heinous crime this time was not doing my homework or not handing it in on time. The upshot was extra homework and standing on a stool again. My problem was I was starting to dislike him and thus the subject at the same time. I'm sure I was not alone. He just didn't explain things very well I thought, particularly when it came to chemical equations. To my surprise I found my father quite sympathetic as he knew Sweet Fanny Adams about chemistry. He suggested that we visit a good bookshop down town and perhaps bought a textbook that was easier to follow. Of course I went along with the idea and so next Saturday was purchased the equivalent of 'An Idiot's Guide to Chemistry and Equations.' It was a revelation. It was made to look so simple it wasn't true. It was actually an American publication and was a big colourful book with lots of illustrations a bit like say the Beano Annual. Within a couple of weeks I think I knew the chemical symbol for almost every element in the Periodic Table, how they combined to form simple chemical compounds and perhaps most importantly why they combined in the proportions that they did. It was a revelation. It wasn't long before it was either my hand, or Cliff Dive's, going up in the class to answer questions. I never let on to Lawrence that Dad had bought me another book and I got my own back at the end of the summer term.

Back to politics. If we thought things were bad in Hong Kong then forty miles to the west, on the other side of the Pearl River estuary, it was sheer bedlam. The Portuguese enclave of Macau was in a state of almost total civil disobedience. It had been a trading post of Portugal since the mid sixteenth century, some three hundred years before Britannia had ventured this way. Whilst the Brits had been securing parts of Gaul and other important territories like the Isle of Wight and the Scilly Isles, her oldest ally Portugal, had looked to Africa and the Orient to extend its influence and increase its wealth. They had given the island of Taiwan its former name of Formosa meaning 'beautiful.'

Macau was a different kettle of fish to Hong Kong and fearful of a Chinese invasion the Government in Lisbon virtually surrendered to the wishes of the Communists when the units of the Portuguese Army failed to quell the violence. In effect political control was given to Peking thirty years before the official handover in the Nineties. Sir David Trench was adamant this was not going to happen in Hong Kong. However the situation continued to deteriorate and just to make matters a whole lot more uncomfortable it stopped raining. Those Easter downfalls had filled every reservoir in the Colony but by about May, when it usually starts to get wet and humid, only the sun followed the usual path of nature. No more picnics were cancelled due to 'inclement weather' and the low pressure contours on the TV charts just simply disappeared.

CHAPTER 9

The weather, and the political climate, was getting hotter. Minor civil disturbances were becoming more widespread and violent and when the TV news started to describe them as 'riots' you just knew the game was changing. The agitators were becoming bolder and brasher. Needless to say that on May Day, when Communists worldwide celebrate Revolution, there were more riots than usual but the Police were well prepared.

At least one of those playground rumours came true with the arrival in the Colony of HMS *Bulwark*, a former fixed-wing carrier that had been converted to a Commando carrier with over six hundred Royal Marines embarked. From memory I think it was 42 Commando. It proved to be a morale booster to a lot of people. I knew somebody who knew somebody who was a crew member and a few of us were lucky enough to get a visit on board her one Saturday morning. It wasn't nearly as impressive as the carrier USS *Shangri La* that I had been aboard in Malta five years earlier but *Bulwark* was still a potent military force and enough for the communist Ta Kung Pau to feature on the front page with the banner headline 'Gunboat Diplomacy.' Somebody obviously didn't like us but the real deterrent was not to arrive for a few months.

It was the end of May and it still hadn't rained.

The Communist owned Bank of China was the tallest building in the central business district and sadly, from a propaganda viewpoint, was considerably taller than the head office of the Hongkong and Shanghai Banking Corporation which was immediately next door. The Communists took full advantage of this and rigged up very powerful microphones on the roof facing in all directions. Thus anybody within several hundred yards was lambasted with non stop chanting of anti-western songs and screams of 'Imperialist Running Dog' and at a decibel level guaranteed to irritate the shit out of even the most constipated of passers by. Worse still one of the microphones boomed out directly towards the lush green pastures of the HK Cricket Club only a hundred yards away. When a full scale riot erupted at the bottom of Garden Road outside the Hilton Hotel one Saturday afternoon things got very bad indeed. Tear gas was fired as were rubber bullets. Some of the rioters were seen emptying small phials of pigs blood onto their torsos to make it look as if they had been shot by British Imperialists and propaganda photographs were taken as such, no doubt for publication in the following day's Chinese papers both in Hong Kong and over the border. The HK Police held firm and knew that fully armed troops were only a few hundred yards away in Victoria Barracks should they be needed to be called upon. But there was one particular propaganda photograph that eclipsed them all and it was one of ours. Believe it or not a routine Saturday afternoon cricket match was taking place less than two hundred yards from the main riot. It was protected by the Club's high wire fence that was supposed to stop well struck balls colliding with a passing Shau Ki Wan tram. On that day alone its role was very different. Next day's South China Morning Post had a photo on the front page depicting normal play in the foreground with a smoke filled riot on the other side of the fence in the background. The caption read something like 'Worst riot yet but meanwhile play continues.' It was this picture, I believe, that convinced many Communists that this was one battle they might just lose.

Security was beefed up all round the Colony when several home made bombs went off in public places. Two innocent young kids were killed in an explosion in a playground. The bombs were disguised as brightly coloured parcels and the local press dubbed them 'pineapple bombs' and warnings were issued to all schools. A traffic cop was killed whilst directing traffic from a small bandstand type structure at a major junction near Star Ferry on the Island and another European police officer lost a leg in another explosion. Where was all the explosive coming from? The border was sealed as tight as a drum and the only refugees making it across were those risking the sharks in Mirs Bay to the east of the main border line. Many didn't make it or lost a limb in the process. All fireworks were suddenly declared illegal as it was realised that the gunpowder contained in them was a likely source of material for the home made devices. Smuggling from Macau was also probably another rich source as at the time Macau was the centre of the biggest firework factories in the world. Many years later a huge explosion in one of them blew half a mountain away. It was not possible to police all the marine traffic in the Pearl Delta estuary as by general consensus, never mind Maritime Law, most of the waterway was 'International' and did not come under the jurisdiction of either Britain, China or Portugal. You could have put the entire Royal Navy, which in 1967 was a considerable size, in the western approaches to Hong Kong and made not one jot of difference. But the 'Andrew' did prove its worth later on.

It was the end of June and still it hadn't rained. Levels in reservoirs were sinking fast and the Government decided to introduce strict water rationing. No doubt it would lead to more civilian unrest and bad feeling but there was little option. Hong Kong consumed more water than it caught from rainfall and the discrepancy was made up by buying water, millions of gallons of it, from China every year via an aqueduct system that was only turned on annually, in September from memory. However, so bad were relations with the authorities on the Mainland that nobody knew if the deal would be honoured. With little or no Government who do you negotiate with? Peking...er no way. The Red Guards? The militia? If so which faction? It was a conundrum that was impossible to answer. Meanwhile contingency plans were put into place to ship millions of gallons to Hong Kong by tanker from Singapore if necessary. The whole Territory was split up into four geographical sectors lettered A, B, C and D and maps were printed in every newspaper to clearly demonstrate which sector you were in. Unbelievably the water was only turned on for four hours every four days per sector. I remember we were in Zone D which covered all of Stanley, indeed most of the southern part of the Island. As you might imagine there was a mad scramble to buy absolutely anything that would literally hold water and, market forces being what they are in capitalist Hong Kong, the prices of buckets and plastic containers of every description went through the roof. As water had to be boiled before it was drunk we set up a veritable water purification plant in the kitchen. Filling everything practical with water during the four hour window we then boiled in kettles gallons of the stuff and then decanted it into many empty Gordons gin bottles which we had saved just for this purpose. About six at a time were then placed in the 'door' section of the huge fridge which I seem to recall was a Whirlpool make. Sometime that summer human error crept in and an almost full bottle of real gin was accidentally put into the fridge. Coming back from school one day and feeling thirsty I quickly made myself a lime juice cordial with the nearest bottle to hand, removed several lumps of ice from one of those awful plastic cube trays and swallowed hard. I nearly hit the roof! I had to confess of course as the gin bottle was now half empty. I think Mum and Dad drank an awful lot of gin and lime over the next few days. The longer this rationing went on the more miserable people got and coupled with the ongoing civil disturbances life in the Colony was not exactly a bed of roses. In fact people started to pong, the exact opposite of roses. The only upside was that swimming pools were temporarily closed including the awful one at Kai Tak for which I reserved a particular dislike. More Gloster Javelin jet fighters had arrived from Singapore in the shape of 60 Squadron giving further proof that Army school playground chatter could compete with Chinese whispers any day. That pool must look like a permanent rainbow now with the amount of aviation fuel in the air. Maybe the toxic fuel would kill all the verruca spores that lurked in its depths. I had already suffered from one and been given a foul liquid called gentian violet to apply to the offending growth on my right foot. Suffering from a verruca was about the only way you could legitimately avoid a swimming class but Fergusson always demanded 'a letter from the MO' or he didn't allow you any leeway.

But don't let me give you the impression that life in Hong Kong at that time was all riots and water rationing. It wasn't. Life still went on and the vast majority of people adopted the British stiff upper lip attitude. The HK Government stepped up its own propaganda war still further and invited organisations to publicly demonstrate their support for 'Law and Order in the Colony' by signing a Register to indicate as such. It started as a trickle at first slowly but shortly, day by day, the number started to swell. They included schools, charities, colleges and even individuals who were not frightened to stick their necks out in the face of continuing insults and accusations of being 'Imperialist lackies' from the loud but increasingly outnumbered leftists. The 'man on the Shau Ki Wan tram' was finding his voice. It was just seeming to look as if the situation was starting to ease when, in the first week of July, matters took a major turn for the worse. It was as violent as it was unexpected and it took the whole Colony by surprise.

On the morning of 8th July, and I know it was a weekend because I was off school, units of communist Red Guards swarmed across the border with China and attacked three police posts with heavy machine guns. There were half a dozen fatalities. It was a game changer. Was this the precursor for a full scale invasion? Was it an isolated incident and down to over zealous local militia? Did it have the blessing and backing of Peking? If it did we were all going to be in serious trouble. The Governor doubtless took immediate advice from London and advised his military commanders on the ground accordingly. Had the insurgents deliberately chosen a weekend in the knowledge that the British Foreign Secretary was in all probability not in London? It is easy to forget that communications in those days were nothing like today. No emails. No computers. No smart phones.

In any event by mid-afternoon several thousand Ghurkhas, perhaps the most loyal units in the British Army's order of battle, had dug in within a mile of the border. It was a good job we had completed our driving course at Dills Corner the year before as the whole frontier area became a no mans' land. What took place in the background wasn't even revealed in the Cabinet Papers traditionally made public thirty years after the event. More troops were flown up from Singapore and possibly even Brunei and the garrison was probably up to ten thousand troops. And the biggest deterrent of all moved at 'best possible speed' north from her base at Sembawang Dockyard. Completed eleven years earlier by Vickers Shipbuilders & Engineering at Barrow in Furness, *HMS Hermes* was Britain's permanently stationed carrier East of Suez. There was no great fanfare on her arrival in port. There didn't need to be. She was just there and highly visible. On board and visible on deck were eight Blackburn Buccaneer strike bombers. Each one was capable of carrying a Red Beard nuclear weapon and could drop it onto a sixpence anywhere within a thousand nautical miles. And that, to me at least, was why Premier Chou En Lai disapproved of any plans to invade Hong Kong by his hot blooded Generals. He could well have ended up with eight 'Hiroshimas' on his hands. That's what you call deterrence. Helicopters operating from *Hermes* dropped Marines onto the roofs of tall buildings suspected of harbouring terrorists in a very public demonstration of naval support. They found caches of weapons, explosives and a makeshift hospital to receive casualties. It was the beginning of the end of the emergency and from then on the Communists knew they had been beaten. Leftist bookshops continued to sell the Thoughts of Chairman Mao Tse Tung, universally known as the Little Red Book, but the number of people waving them about in the air shouting leftist slogans stared to diminish. Some 'Imperialist Running Dogs' bought one as a souvenir. I did and believe it or not I still have it. Printed in 1966 it is a genuine first edition with a monochrome picture of Mao himself inside the front cover and delicately protected with a sheet of transparent rice paper. It's probably worth a few quid on e-Bay but I'll think I'll keep it to remind me of those crazy, crazy days in 1967.

CHAPTER 10

On the plus side I managed to scrape through the end of year exams, well in most subjects anyway. I was now in the 'top set' for Maths along with five others including a Ghurkha chappie called Rohit Thapa, the son of a Warrant Officer stationed at Sek Kong in the New Territories. Mike was the other male and Sandra, Sally and Diana were the three girls.

Latin was just awful, again, and of course I got very low marks as expected. With luck I would be able to drop it as the Latin teacher was going back to UK. My French was good and I can recall an amusing moment one day in class. Two new boys had arrived in school from Belfast – twins called Eric and Colin Smith. Their father worked at a place called Gilnahirk, a GCHQ station in Ulster. They were nice lads but never having travelled outside the Province, their accents were so thick you could have cut them with a bread knife. This presented great difficulties to the Clydeside born Miss McDade who could barely understand a word they said. Translating a passage about shopping in class one day one of them, I can't remember which, got stuck for a word and raised his hand to attract the lady's attention.

'Yes, Smith, what is is?'

'Please Muss, what's Ay-Uggs?'

'I beg your pardon.'

'What's French for Ay-Uggs, Muss?'

I was sat behind Smith and volunteered my assistance. 'He means eggs, Miss. He wants to know the French word for eggs.'

I had very quickly learnt that unique amongst the English speaking peoples those from Northern Ireland have developed a penchant for splitting some short single syllable words into two even shorter words. Hence eggs becomes *Ay-Uggs*. Likewise a Mercedes Benz becomes a Mercedes *Bay-Unz*. It is most odd but OK once you get used to it you soon become bilingual so to speak. Miss McDade never did get used to it but there again she didn't have to as her tour of duty in Hong Kong had also come to an end. The universally disliked Fergusson was replaced by a nice chap called Alan Jones so, for me at least, that was a plus. I would no longer be called 'Sheehy' who by coincidence had also hailed from Gilnahirk.

My English Language marks were acceptable and I could write a good essay. I had surprised my teacher, Elwyn Roberts, one day when he had gone round the entire class one at a time and asked us what book we were currently reading. As if you had the time! There were titters of laughter when an attempt at humour was made.

'The Little Red Book, Sir' was Gerald Simpson's reply. 'Thank you, Simpson, that's quite enough. You will learn nothing, boy.' 'A Winter's Tale, Sir, to remind me of home here in Hong Kong' was another response.

And finally Roberts got to me the last one as I was sat furthest away from him.

'I'm reading a book of short stories, Sir, by V.S. Pritchett.' Roberts was stunned.

'Really, Harland? I'm amazed, boy. Is there any particular story that stands out? If so what is its title?'

'Yes, Sir. It's called *The Skirt*.' The whole class dissolved into laughter. Except Mr Roberts of course who had just been upstaged by me albeit unintentionally. Fortunately for me the bell rang and that was the end of the class.

The American Chemistry book had transformed my ability in that subject and unbelievably I came second in the class in the end of year exam. I think Lawrence was shocked too but he had the good grace to mutter 'well done Harland' when he handed the marked papers back to us. I decided to do Chemistry the following year and take it up to 'O' level as it was a straight choice in the timetable to do either Chemistry or History. Sadly it was also a straight choice between Biology and Physics. This proved to be a dilemma that was not easy to resolve as I wanted to do both. In the event I dropped Biology which later proved to be the wrong choice as I ended up doing 'A' level not having passed the subject at 'O' level.

The bottom line was that I was heading for Form 4A and not Year 4 at Scarborough College after all. Phew! We said goodbye to quite a few classmates whose fathers were being transferred to other parts of the Empire or back to UK. These included the awfully English sounding Richard Ribchester, John 'Jumbo' Dennis, my cricketing partner Gareth Pearce and Gerald Simpson who lived not far from us in Stanley Mound Road. We went to see Gerald, his brother Karl (their mother was German hence the spelling) and his parents off at Kai Tak Airport. They were lucky enough to be flying in one of the brand spanking new Vickers VC10 aircraft, a squadron of which had been purchased by the Ministry of Defence for RAF Transport Command. By co-incidence our Headmaster, P.A. Croft MA (Cantab) was also seeing off a colleague on the same flight, quite possibly another teacher. For some reason Gerald was carrying a short walking stick and hat as if he was 'Singing in the Rain' like Gene Kelly and just before he went through the departure gate he faced Mr Croft and waiving the hat and stick in the air said 'Toodle pip old chap. You didn't know I was leaving did you?' Like Queen Victoria, Croft was not amused as he and Gerald had had many a contretemps during the previous two years. I was sorry also to say goodbye to a lovely fair haired girl called Cynthia Wilkinson, the daughter of an Army Sergeant, having taken quite a shine to her during the year.

Some good news arrived courtesy of the 1st Battalion the Welch Regiment. They ran the Yacht Club at St. Stephens Bay in Stanley and were offering a month long training course for novices during the summer holiday. The typical Army memo read similarly to the Driving Course memo from the previous year:

'Places are limited. Those interested should put their names forward without delay etc...'

I jumped at the chance. This was more like it. The Course would occupy four weeks of the six week holiday and as St. Stephens Beach was only fifteen minutes walk away from Gordon Terrace it was just perfect. I was joined by Leigh Davies and 'Bazza' Cuthbert, both St. Georges pupils who also lived in Gordon Terrace.

Predictably and inevitably more 'Joining Instructions' arrived from the Army: 'Registration on Day 1 will take place at O-eight hundred etc....' I couldn't wait for the day to arrive and it was probably about 20th July.

CHAPTER 11

The Officer in Charge was one Lieutenant Davies who spoke with more than a slight Welsh lilt as you might imagine. A Register had been drawn up which, typical of the Army, was in alphabetical order. He ticked our names off one at a time, about twenty from memory. Some fifty yards away lying half in and half out of the water were six sailing dinghies all in parallel like beached dolphins waiting for a Japanese dinner plate. At each one was a squaddie, presumably an instructor, waiting for his crew. Within five minutes we had been assigned to one of the six boats in groups of three or four. Cuthbert was in my group along with two young Aussie chaps who looked about twelve. Ends out they were twin brothers, newly arrived from Oz and the sons of one Squadron Leader Sandy Baxter RAAF.

We all jumped into the boat only to be bellowed at by our instructor who was known only as Frank.

'And how the fxxxx do you think the boat's going to get onto the water with you 'orrible lot in it, Boyos?'

So we all got out and slowly pushed the boat, known as an Enterprise, out into waist deep water. Then we jumped in. It was a long slow job. Learning first how to lower the centreboard which kept the boat on an even keel in a breeze, slot on the huge tiller and finally hoist the mainsail followed by the jib. It was hot, very hot and I was glad I had brought a shirt as I still burnt easily in the height of summer. We sailed round and round the Bay which was probably about a mile in diameter. It seemed most odd at first to get a view of our flats from the sea. You looked at the whole Stanley Peninsular from a very different perspective. We came back ashore for lunch and munched on sandwiches we had brought with us, swigged on bottles of Coke bought from a kiosk and chatted to pals who had been allocated to different boats. In the afternoon we did more of the same but each of us in turn was given the tiller for spells of about twenty minutes to get the feel of the boat. We did turns to the left and right to take different 'tacks' in the wind giving the correct verbal signals as we did so. It was 'ready about lee ho' if you pushed the tiller away from you and 'ready about gybe ho' if the tiller was pulled towards you. It took time to get used to the main boom swinging towards you which you had to duck under or a bump and a thick head was coming your way. By about four in the afternoon it was time to bring the first day to a close. I think it was Bazza who was invited to take the tiller as we headed for the beach.

'Just steer it in a straight line onto the sand between those other two boats, Boyo.'

So he did. Big mistake. We all fell over as the centreboard buried itself into the soft sand and brought the whole boat to a sudden halt as though somebody had stood on disc brakes. It had been quite deliberate on Frank's part.

'And that's what 'appens, Boyo, when you forget to raise the centreboard before you hit the beach. Don't do it again 'orright, Boyo.'

And so ended the first lesson. Over tea at home I suspect that quite a few parents were keen to ask how their offspring had fared on Day 1 of the twenty day course. I was most enthusiastic and looking forward to the remaining nineteen days.

On the eastern side of the Stanley Peninsular about a mile away as the Red Kite flies (there are no crows in Hong Kong) was the largest gaol in the Territory. It is called simply 'Stanley Prison' and it had a truly shocking history. It is approached by heading south through the village on the only main road which then, just past the Police Station, forks right for St. Stephens and Stanley Fort or left for Stanley Prison which is sited at the end of a very long Tung Tau Wan Road. On a day when it is not too hot it is a most pleasant twenty minute walk. The first building on your left is the Catholic St. Anne's Church of fairly modern construction, certainly post-War. On Sundays you could hear its bells ringing just as you might hear a village church's bells anywhere in rural England. Past the church, also on the left, was sited the Hong Kong Sea School. Paddy had told us much about it on the long voyage from London and he was obviously well acquainted with its educational reputation. It was 'boys only' for young men from a poor background interested in a life in the Merchant Navy or marine careers generally. There were two main teaching blocks painted brilliant white which you could see from miles away in the brilliant sunshine. The extensive grounds extended right down to the water's edge with slipways for boats allowing access. There was also a mock ship's mast from which lanyards flew flags and ensigns, no doubt to teach every pupil the skills of signalling in the old fashioned way. For example if you flew a red flag with a triangular chunk cut out on the right hand side then flown alone (as the letter B) it meant 'Bugger off you tosser, I'm unloading explosives! Very useful indeed I'm sure. Competition was fierce to join the school and there were probably several hundred pupils at any one time. The boys were easily recognisable with their HKSS shirts and motif. I am not sure how it was funded but many British Flagged vessels sailing to and from the Far East would have had crew who were educated there and I would not be surprised if they had not in some degree contributed funds.

Walking on past the Sea School there are luxury houses and villas all with magnificent views of Tai Tam Bay and the Cape D'Aguilar peninsula about two miles to the east which was mountainous and forested but unlike Stanley was almost totally unpopulated. The first indication of a Prison you see is a military style barrier with a guard hut which was wooden and the sole function of which was to provide the duty guard with shade. It was almost casual in style and belied what was beyond. To the left were a few apartment blocks for housing both local and expatriate staff and then, all on its own, was a white painted two storey building that reeked of a colonial past. Its official name was the Prison Officers Sports Club but it was known simply as The Stanley Club and a quaint almost pub- like wooden sign swung on two short chains over the main entrance. Beyond the Club was a small car park and if you followed the road straight on you came to it about two hundred yards distant. Stanley Prison itself. Ahead of you was a white concrete wall at least thirty feet tall with a main door of the type that you see prisoners emerging from after so many years porridge, or rice in this case. The whole of the main security area was surrounded on all four sides with this huge wall. Forget Holloway or Wormwood Scrubs. This was Hong Kong's Colditz. It housed murderers, Triad members, narcotics dealers (local and international) and every type of crim you could think of. The whole shebang probably measured four hundred yards by two hundred. Although Great Britain had abolished capital punishment many of her Colonies and Dependencies had not and hangings were fairly frequent events. I was to meet several of the qualified hangmen personally over the following few years.

Just before our first Christmas in Hong Kong in 1966 a member of the Stanley Club invited our family to attend the annual Prison Fair held at a weekend. This was a new one. A prison fair? We parked the Cortina somewhere outside the first barrier and walked to the Club where our hosts met us. Walking on foot towards the main gate we turned left towards some sports fields which were just heaving with people. It was indeed like a fairground but minus the dodgems and roller coaster. There were coconut shies and games galore and everyone was having a great time. We learned that this annual event was to raise funds for prisoner's welfare after they had (hopefully) been assimilated back into civilised society. Quite how you go about assimilating a millionaire international heroin dealer and convert him into being a corner shop owner I never did find out. I guess the idea was right in principle. There was lots of produce to buy too, all made by the prisoners in workshops inside the secure area. We bought two wooden and rattan stools each about eighteen inches square and a foot high. They were very useful for changing light bulbs when you couldn't quite reach the fitments dangling from the ceiling. Believe it or not they are both still in my possession fifty years later. The most impressive items on sale though were undoubtedly paintings all painted by prisoners too. Surprisingly they were not all of traditional Oriental scenes and two, of what looked like North American forest scenes, were particularly eye catching. Every stall was manned by a uniformed prison officer and Dad made enquiries. The two paintings in question, he said, were painted by an international heroin dealer who had lived in British Columbia, Canada prior to being extradited back to Hong Kong to face charges and subsequent lengthy imprisonment. Dad bought the two pictures, perhaps just as much because of the story as the artistic talent they portrayed. Likewise, I still have them.

It wasn't long before Dad became an Associate member of the Stanley Club in his own right. The access to social facilities would be very nice, especially for Mum, as lots of ladies used the Club for weekly gatherings on Library Nights particularly. It did indeed have a well stocked library of both fiction and non-fiction and this was something Mum missed very much overseas. Like her own mother before her she was an avid reader and borrower from Scarborough Library and this would make up somewhat for her loss. The two main attractions for Dad were the bowling green and the Bar.

In England lawn bowls is a game played by elderly men wearing grey flannels, white jumpers and flat brown shoes in such places as Much Binding in the Marsh, Little Twittleton and Eastbourne. They break in the 15C heat for tea and freshly made lemonade and when the match is over they shake hands, drink more tea, eat fruit cake and discuss their latest maladies until it is time to go home to 'her indoors' and suffer hours of earache before watching Panorama and then going to bed.

It wasn't like that in Hong Kong.

In Hong Kong there was a League of Three Divisions and it was so competitive you would not believe it. With at least two dozen clubs all situated within an hour's travelling time of each other skills were practised and honed to a degree higher than anywhere else in the world. As proof Hong Kong would take many a gold medal at Commonwealth level. Many Companies, known as 'Hongs' in the Colony had their own Clubs, greens and teams. The HK Electric Company was just one of them. Other Clubs were dual sports clubs such as the HK Cricket Club which had its own bowls greens, as did the Craigengower C.C. in Happy Valley which as I mentioned before was near the Naval apartments at Harcourt Place. So why was the gentlemanly sport of lawn bowls so different in Hong Kong?

The answer, in one word, is drink. Not tea but beer, lots and lots of beer. Usually the locally brewed San Miguel but often Carling Black label and occasionally exotic imports like Amstel, Carlsberg and Tuborg. Dad was particularly partial to a Tuborg, a Danish brew with a gold foil top which you removed first before taking the top off. A bit like a champagne bottle I suppose. You didn't break for 'tea' in Hong Kong. At each end of the green were wooden 'pigeon holes' where club waiters would keep you topped up throughout the match. You needed to replace the liquid lost through perspiration after all and also remember that in Hong Kong bowls is a game played in the hot, humid summer when it rains. The clover grass comprising most clubs' manicured greens dried out and went brown in Hong Kong's arid winter.

Dad learnt to play the game and became quite good, taking part in friendly matches with some of the Prison Officers after work in mid-week and at weekends. Over the years many of these Officers became friends of the family and there were some very interesting characters amongst them. Most of them were British but having lived overseas for so long, some of them since WW2, the long three month leave back to UK was often referred to as 'going away' rather than 'going home' such was their attachment to Hong Kong. Many had Chinese wives including one Andy Salmon who had unfortunately been a Prisoner of War in Stanley during the terrible years of the Japanese Occupation. His son, Kenny, became a firm friend of mine over many years and he became a DJ and presenter on University Radio Essex. I remember lending him a '45' single called Classical Gas by Mason Williams as he wanted to record it as the signature tune for his programme. I hope he is alive and well wherever he is in the world today. Some of the senior Prison Officers were Asian, mainly Punjabi I believe, and some of them were also great bowlers including one B. Singh who was a brilliant Number Three, the best I have ever seen anywhere. To those of you who don't understand bowls the last player to put down his woods is the 'Skip' but if he doesn't have a good Number Three to direct him then he might as well play blindfolded. B. Singh would throw his sweat towel onto the grass and boom out:

'I want it here! You must be UP!

That last reference meant the Skip must not be short and must be UP with the jack. Woe betide the Skip if he fell short and if he did then the bilingual B. Singh would bark an order to a waiter to top up the Skip's glass. He obviously wasn't drinking enough!

Several of the senior Officers were also trained hangmen and were called upon to do that duty whenever the Governor, who had ultimate sanction, declined to reprieve the condemned. I know the names of some of them but it would not be fair to reveal them in this book. One of them had an absolutely stunning Eurasian daughter who was subsequently married to a well known British actor. If she ever reads this book I hope she gets in touch. I still treasure the Stanley Club tie her father gave me many years later.

CHAPTER 12

The summer holidays drew to a close and we fortunately had some relief from the water rationing. A few big Tropical Storms in the South China Sea brought some welcome rainfall. As I recall we did not get any direct hits, let alone any full blooded typhoons, but very often these cyclonic storms brought heavy rain 'in the tail' as they swept westwards into Hainan island or the coast of North Vietnam. And speaking of Vietnam it was becoming obvious that the military situation in the whole of Indochina was deteriorating markedly. Thousands more GIs were heading west from the USA and this was reflected in the number and frequency of US Navy ships that were calling into Hong Kong en route to patrols off the Vietnamese coast.

Civilian strife in the Colony which had been disrupting the lives of many as they went about their normal lives started to tail off. There was the odd sporadic disturbance but they were contained and localised. Overall there had been over twenty deaths including an Army Bomb Disposal expert who was killed on active duty and a radio journalist who was attacked and killed in his car. Eventually, towards the end of the year, an order seemingly came from on high in Peking that organised violence was to end. It wasn't just politics, it was money. China earned the vast majority of its foreign exchange via the Bank of China in Hong Kong and who would want to kill the golden goose? Or even the golden crispy duck?!

School recommenced in September and went up a year into Class 4A. We had sadly said goodbye to many classmates but now it was time to welcome new ones. They included one Steve Ryan who came to live in Reef Court in Stanley. He was keen on fishing, like me, and we spent many an hour angling from the rocks at St. Stephens and Stanley Beach. Some new teachers arrived from UK and other Army Schools including a Mr Gareth Evans who was my new form teacher and who also taught Physics. Biology was dropped with mixed blessings. I did not take to my new English teacher who placed more importance on literature than language. Thus introductions to Thomas Hardy, Chaucer and Shakespeare did not go down well. However even this caused some mirth one day when I was suffering at home with a very high temperature and a Medical Officer was summoned from the clinic at Stanley Fort. He was very broad Welsh as you might expect with the Welch Regiment garrisoned there. He examined me and grinned as he took one look at the textbook by my bedside. It was 'The Mayor of Casterbridge' by Thomas Hardy.

'A bit heavy that book, Boyo. No wonder you're feeling ill, Boyo. I'd give it a rest if I were you, Boyo.'

So I did, permanently. I simply hated doing English Literature. To have to study it anywhere, let alone in cosmopolitan and vibrant Hong Kong, was a dreadful chore. I put it in the same category as Latin. There was bad news on that front too. A new Latin teacher arrived from London and I was somehow persuaded to carry on with it for at least another year. The good news was that the teacher, a Mr David Hall, was a very nice man indeed which at least sweetened the pill slightly. A new pupil also joined the Latin class in the shape of the gorgeous Joan Partridge. Joan's father was British Army and her mother was of African descent and this mixed race young lady was an absolute stunner. As I recall she was particularly good at Latin and English. Better than me anyway. Miss McDade departed the Colony and our French lessons were now fume free of Chanel, Avon or whatever. She was replaced by an Englishman, a Mr Rich, whose son John was also a class mate. I didn't mind doing French as at least, unlike Latin, it was a world language although not quite as useful as I thought as I discovered two years later in Montreal.

My new Chemistry teacher was non other than the Deputy Head, Miss 'Cleo Lane' Gilbert. She proved to be very good indeed and with at least half the former class choosing the alternative of History we were down to about fifteen pupils in the class. I recall that she was always worried about chlorine gas seeping from apparatus and reacting with the plethora of silver rings that she wore. She was paranoid about it but I rather liked Miss Gilbert and my Chemistry got even better. Cliff Dive and I were by far the best two in the Class and I wanted to see if I could 'pip' him to top of the class in next year's exam. I didn't get the chance as the Dive family left for the UK, I think in the November.

Dependent on rank, service, size of your cap etc. many GCHQ families had the opportunity to travel back to UK by sea at the end of their three year tour of duty. Compensation for the gruelling thirty-six hour brain numbing flight by turbo-prop was a four week voyage, usually but not always, on one of P & O's great white liners. In the sixties there were half a dozen of these elegant vessels still plying the 'Orient run' and it wasn't called Peninsular and Oriental Steam Navigation Company for nothing. *Oronsay*, like the aircraft carrier HMS *Hermes*, was also built by Vickers Armstrong at Barrow in Furness demonstrating the skills and adaptability of that great company. It was customary for all departing passengers on these liners to be given 'guest passes' so that friends could be entertained on board in the final few hours before sailing. Thus Cliff managed to squeeze a couple of these passes from his parents to allow Mike and I aboard. How exciting.

I remember that the departure time was very late at night, possibly around midnight, and as this was during the week, arrangements were made for me to stay overnight at Mike's place at Conduit Road in Mid-Levels and to go to school with him on his school bus the following morning. It was indeed a great send off and P & O always did the job properly with a band playing despite the lateness of the hour. I think we got the last ferry back to Hong Kong Island where Bob had left the Zodiac in the car park near Star Ferry. Those departures were always quite emotional as you never knew when you would see your friend again, if ever. The girls always cried.

Once again summer had turned to Autumn and we morphed from summer to winter school uniforms. As if our days were not long enough already the Army introduced new 'activity hours' and the more astute amongst us realised that there was almost certainly another reason lurking behind this, probably a shortage of buses. So you had to make a choice of what 'activity' to pursue after normal school hours but to be honest the choice was fairly limited. I opted for boat building which was to be headed by one Mr Davies a sports teacher who was, it seems, also a keen yachtsman. The project involved building an *Enterprise* class dinghy from scratch, following a master plan with drawings supplied from goodness knows where. The plans were as large as the intended boat itself. I resented the extra hour but I stuck with it for a term at least. Progress was painfully slow I recall. By Christmas the thing still hadn't resembled anything that might float, let alone race. Most of the girls had opted for extra Domestic Science classes i.e. cooking. I'll bet that the majority did not put their skills to practice at home though as the vast majority of Service families had 'amahs' who were locally employed maids, most of whom lived in servants quarters built into most expatriates' living quarters. Actually though, we didn't have an amah. Mum didn't go to work like many Mums and wives and in any event she was an excellent cook in her own right and would not have wanted a 'foreigner' in her kitchen. The biggest question then was who was responsible for polishing the great expanse of parquet flooring on a weekly basis? The answer was that Dad and I usually shared that burden on a Saturday morning. The hard wax polish, usually the Mansion brand, was applied by hand to the floor by cloth a square yard at a time and polished off to a shine with an electric Bex Bissell polisher that looked like a hoover with two contra-rotating mops underneath it. With a Gordon Terrace flat covering an area of almost two thousand square feet this was a big job but I was usually rewarded with extra pocket money over and above the usual ten Hong Kong dollars which was about fifteen shillings in old money. This was quite a lot of money in those days but from that we had to pay our Star ferry fares twice daily. Much of my pocket money was spent on newspapers, usually the China Mail for ten cents or if I felt flush the HK Tiger Standard for twenty cents. Even at that age I was becoming a 'news junkie' and when I got home after school I would swap papers with Dad and then read the more authoritative and heavyweight South China Morning Post which was delivered every day by North Point Stores. I guess the SCMP as it was known, was the *Daily Telegraph* of the Far East. Like the *Telegraph* today the SCMP had a business supplement and two daily Sections that always interested me. One concerned shipping, the other aviation.

The shipping section had three columns; ships in port, ships expected and ships departing. It was a Geography lesson every day. Thus entries might read:

'*Benledi*...Ben Line....Berth 6....Kowloon Wharf *Akagi Maru*...Mitsui OSK Lines...Ocean Terminal

Cathay...P & O....from Southampton....Ocean terminal *Hydra*....Blue Funnel Lines....from Liverpool...Holts Wharf

SA African Trader...SAFMARINE...departing for Durban *President Wilson*...President Lines...departing for San Francisco.

How could you not be interested in Geography and Commerce when that information was available in your newspaper every day?

The Aviation column was just as informative. It was split into two long vertical columns, Arrivals on the left, Departures on the right thus:

CX 123 from Tokyo 09:00 QF 234 to Melbourne 08:45 CX 345 from Manila 10:15 SIA 225 to Singapore 09:05

And so forth right through the day until about eleven at night when the last flights departed, usually for Europe to fit in with early morning arrivals at London Heathrow, Frankfurt etc. The last two flights out were nearly always the BOAC flight to London and the famous round the world flight by PanAm also heading for London and then on to JFK New York.

So if you say wanted to meet a friend who you knew was arriving on a certain flight number you just picked up that day's SCMP and planned accordingly. Today of course you would go online with your smart phone, i-pad or whatever to check on arrivals but it all seemed so important when the flights were listed in a newspaper. I will tell you a little later about a special flight I had to meet in January the following year.

Hong Kong Airport, or more specifically, Kai Tak International, was a marvel of civil engineering. There had been an 'airfield' in Kowloon since the 20s which had been built for the Royal Air Force. There was never enough flat land on Hong Kong Island so from an engineering viewpoint the choice was limited to say the least. The original 'air strip' was on the east side of Kowloon roughly parallel to the coast but when commercial aviation started to arrive in a big way in the Fifties this proved totally inadequate. A new runway some eight thousand feet long was constructed jutting out into Kowloon Bay in a south easterly direction like a giant jetty. For the aviation buffs amongst you the runway orientation was 13/31. The downside was that when wind directions demanded it an aircraft's approach had to be from the north west and over some pretty tricky high terrain (one of the nine dragons) necessitating a major turn to starboard at very low altitude and less than a mile from touchdown. Thus the legend of the 'hair raising' landing at Kai Tak was born and some readers might remember it being depicted in the movie 'The Chairman' starring Gregory Peck, the chairman in question being Mao Tse Tung. Accidents did happen at Kai Tak as you might expect. In fact I remember two alone in 1967. A Cathay Pacific Convair Coranado failed to lift off properly on take off and powered off the end of the runway ending up in the drink in Kowloon Bay. One passenger, an American lady I think, died from a heart attack. I do remember the pilot being interviewed on radio very soon afterwards with the words:

'One fatality in over a hundred passengers. That's not bad.'

The plane was a write-off. Coronados were airliners built by Convair near San Diego, California and named after the district which shelters the giant naval base from the Pacific Ocean. They were a very under-rated plane and although smaller then their contemporaries were faster than a 707 or a DC8 and could outpace and overtake them on the Hong Kong to Tokyo route much to the chagrin of Cathay Pacific's rivals.

The other accident that year was much more serious. A Thai International Caravelle airliner crashed into Kowloon Bay about a mile short of the runway in very bad weather caused by a Tropical Storm. The tail section broke off and sank. Over twenty souls were lost and it was a grim day for Hong Kong aviation. It was about this time that consideration was initially given to greatly lengthening the runway at Kai Tak from eight thousand feet to twelve thousand feet. Safety was given as the main reason but the first flight of Boeing's 'Jumbo Jet' the 747 was only two years away and any international airport that couldn't handle this mammoth of the skies would lose out commercially to those that could.

That term at school was largely uneventful. Christmas was soon upon us again, our second in the Colony but some time late in that year we moved flats within Gordon Terrace from Number 8 to Number 4 which was only about sixty yards but the difference was amazing. The old flat faced due east but the new one south west and caught all the afternoon and evening sunshine. More importantly though it faced the right direction for sea breezes, especially at night, which minimised the use of air-conditioning units in bedrooms. We were assisted in the move by the resident caretaker,

Ah Hoy, a happy Chinaman in his fifties who lived in an outhouse with his wife and son. He had arranged to hire four additional men he knew in the village and a daily rate of twenty dollars a day per head was agreed in advance. The men arrived about eight in the morning and started carrying furniture and everything we owned or hired, first down two flights of stairs, then half-way around the roundabout that characterised Gordon Terrace, across a forecourt then up two more flights of stairs to our new flat. Dad was having kittens as he watched progress from the balcony of the new flat. There were several brown trouser moments as a tea chest full of glassware and crockery swung alarmingly between two bamboo poles being carried on the shoulders of two of the coolies. How it didn't swing off and smash into a thousand pieces I'll never know. By about twelve noon it was time for a meal break and Dad gave Ah Hoy twenty dollars to take the men to a 'chow stall' in the village with an extra five bucks for some beer. They were all smiles and returned an hour later even smilier. By five 'o' clock the job was complete. The Chinese chappies had done a grand job and Dad gave them a large red one hundred dollar bill to share out between them plus a packet of fags each. They were over the moon. When they had gone Ah Hoy was rewarded with a fifty dollar bill for the gaffer's role he had played in the operation. He was probably over two moons.

Christmas in our new flat with sunshine and sea breezes was wonderful. The Sheehy family lived in the flat above us but as the dreaded Fergusson had left the Colony I was spared the cry of:

'Sheehy, come here youse!'

CHAPTER 13

Fortunately 1968 was not going to prove as traumatic as the year before. There were no riots, bombs in the streets or dead policemen and soldiers. The rains and thus the water supplies were back to normal. There were though many happenings that enriched my life and which stayed in my memory, as evidenced by this book.

School took on a routine and boredom all of its own. Am I the only person who resented the thousands of hours learning stuff that would not ever be in the slightest bit useful in life? Maths was progressing nicely under John Kotch's excellent tutorship but did you really need to prove the Cosign Rule to get on in the world? What the hell was the Cosign Rule anyway? It was to get much worse a year later but I'll come to that.

Having taken medical advice (from the nice Welsh doctor) that all olde English literature was bad for your health, I gave up on it completely. We were informed however that the whole class would be entered for 'O' level English Language six months earlier than normal thus allowing anybody who failed it to be given the chance to resit it within the normal time frame if necessary. This didn't bother me unduly as I had always been fairly good at comprehension, precis and essays. With luck I would pass it.

French lessons were made interesting and realistic with the opening of the school's so called Language Lab. Quite what experiments and research we were supposed to conduct I'm not sure but I have to say that using it was quite fun. The 'lab' had a master console controlled by the teacher in charge. Every pupil, I think up to about thirty in number, had a sub console at his or her station consisting of a reel to reel tape recorder, all of which were 'in sync' with each other. You had a microphone in front of you like a radio broadcaster. There would be a master tape controlled by the teacher to which you all to listen in. Thus a story might commence:

'Hier, Monsieur Lebrun et sa femme, Natalie, et ses enfants Marc, Jean-Paul et Annelie sont allés á la plage.'

Question: Combien de fils a Monsieur Lebrun? Thirty voices would then answer in unison: 'Il en a deux!' Deuxième question: Comment s'appelle sa fille?' 'Elle s'appelle Annelie.'

And so you get the general drift. It was great fun – for about a week. With practise you could see when the teacher was about to listen to you as he glanced swiftly at you before he pressed the button for your console. This was your cue to sit up sharp, stop looking at the passing Coronado screaming into Kai Tak and lay on your thickest French accent with a straight face. Occasionally you might be rewarded with a click and a buzz followed by the teachers voice thus:

'Très bien Monsieur 'arland. Huit points. Merci.' In that respect it was a bit like Eurovision without having to sing. It was probably just as well I wasn't learning German as the temptation to emulate Hitler or Goebels would have been too good too miss. And as for Latin well somehow I don't think that *Caesar in Gaul* would have sounded quite right in a language lab. When you think about it the whole thing was an under-utilisation of resources as St. Georges could and should have churned out at least fifty fluent Chinese speakers every year. Even Bletchley Park could not have competed with that.

At the end of January our second Chinese New Year arrived. The Year of the Monkey. However the monkeys that actually arrived were dubbed 'Charlie' and were Viet Cong insurgents, millions of who attacked South Vietnam precisely at the Lunar New Year. It was known as the 'Tet Offensive' 'tet' being the Vietnamese word for New Year. All hell broke loose in the whole of Indo-China which had a knock-on effect on the whole of South East Asia for seven years. It was a full scale war just five hundred miles down the road. American President Lyndon Baines Johnson (LBJ) was under increasing pressure to do something. Pentagon sponsored maps of Asia showed a red coloured Vietnam which started to bleed all over the continent as country after country fell under the kosh of advancing communism. Laos, Cambodia, Thailand and even Malaya were under threat from the ever advancing Viet Cong backed up of course by a vociferous Mao Tse Tung chanting 'Power grows out of the barrel of a gun' from his little red book. It was all very unnerving. China was backing North Vietnam and the Viet Cong with money and materiel, big time. More and more warships started to arrive in Hong Kong from the US Seventh Fleet, most base ported in San Diego. Britain played a very clever game politically and Prime Minister Harold Wilson refused to commit British troops but lent verbal support to America. Hong Kong was a mere pimple on the backside of China and as a listening post and watering hole for sailors and airmen on R & R from Vietnam it was invaluable. The numbers of bars and brothels multiplied many times over particularly in the Wan Chai area of Hong

Kong Island. Every time a U.S. carrier arrived with several thousand horny sailors on board, all flush with combat pay, the more money was made. The profits were OK but they also brought venereal diseases including the notorious 'Vietnam Rose' which was said to be incurable with normal antibiotics. We were even warned about it at school. As if my pocket money would stretch to it! The Vietnam War, as it then became known, dominated the news broadcasts in the Colony for many months and it took other major stories or events to knock it off the front page.

We received bad news by telegram towards the end of January. Grandpop, Dad's father, was dangerously ill in a naval hospital in London. This had happened before five years earlier during a previous tour to Malta. Sadly this time it was much more serious and by eleven 'o' clock that same night Dad was on a PanAm 707 heading for London. Sadly Pops passed away a few hours before the plane got into Heathrow. Today he might have made it with non-stop flights on Dreamliners and 777s but in those days no less then five stops were involved which from memory were Bangkok, Delhi, Teheran, Beirut and Frankfurt. Ten days later Dad flew back to Hong Kong with BOAC and we got a message to say that one of his work colleagues, Bill Bradshaw, would collect him at the airport and take him home, arriving at about six in the evening assuming the plane was on time. I went to school as usual that day and looking forward to seeing Dad. He would be feeling sad I knew. The day, or rather the afternoon, did not go according to plan. I was in a Chemistry lesson, the first of the afternoon, when a knock at the door and a sharp 'all rise for the headmaster' signalled that Mr Croft was about to enter the room.

'Thank you be seated. Carry on.'

It was a good job I was not stood on the stool as per the previous year with the bearded Mr Lawrence. Croft went and spoke quietly to Miss Gilbert who then pointed a finger at me to indicate who I was.'

'Harland, I have just received a telephone message to advise you that a Naval Officer is calling to collect you from the school in fifteen minutes time to take you to the airport to meet your father on his return from London. You are excused school for the rest of the day.'

Ten minutes later I found myself outside in Norfolk Road more than a bit puzzled. A naval officer? Maybe I should be looking for a navy blue Land Rover with RN in white letters on the side. I spotted a Ford Cortina further up the road and sat behind the wheel having a fag was my Dad's colleague.

'Hello, Mr Bradshaw, it's a surprise to see you here.'

We had met before. He and and Dad went back a long way. In fact they had joined the Navy together on the same day in 1938 in Chatham and here they both were thirty years later working for the same outfit eight thousand miles away.

'Ah there you are, Mark. Jump in. We're off to Kai Tak to meet your dad.'

'Thanks Mr Bradshaw but I can't. I'm supposed to be waiting for a naval officer.'

'Yes, I phoned the headmaster a while ago and gave my name as Admiral Bradshaw. I knew that would make him jump.'

The BOAC 707 arrived on time and we three were all soon in the Cortina heading for the vehicular ferry at Hung Hom which would take us to the North Point area of Hong Kong Island. There was a huge queue of cars at the ferry terminal and a long wait looked inevitable. Not so. Bill knew the drill and stuck his right hand out of the car window, fingers and thumbs stretched out to demonstrate the number five. Within seconds a uniformed ferry officer trotted up to the car and accepted a five dollar note which Bill produced from his shirt pocket. We were immediately directed to the front of the queue and the chain guarding the last parking place on the stern of the ferry was miraculously uncoupled and on we drove.

'And that's how it's done out here, Vic. It's called tea money and it works.'

Unbelievably and sadly I lost my other grandfather, Walter Jewitt, four months later. Grandad had been a resident in Green Gables Retirement Home since we had left Scarborough in July 1966. He had lived with us for several years following Gran's passing and our large beautiful garden was the result of much of his handiwork as much as Dad's and mine. The pristine exhibition of dahlias and chrysanthemums was entirely due to his green fingers. I had missed my daily chats with him terribly and the fortnightly 'air mail bluey' I sent to him, as promised, was my way of keeping in touch. On the 4th of May I got home from school to find Mum in tears and the Cable and Wireless telegram from her brother Bert laying on the coffee table. It was short and to the point;

'Regret father died. Bert.'

We knew that Grandad had been poorly for a while but even so the bluntness of the message hit you like a rapier. Today we would have spoken, texted, Face-booked and skyped for weeks before the final curtain, so to speak. The courier riding a red motorbike clutching a brown envelope usually meant only one thing. On reading the missive I too filled with tears. It was the end of an era and now for the first time in my life I was without a grandfather.

That year, 1968, was remembered for the many and varied school trips that were organised usually during 'triple Geography' lessons which usually meant a whole morning from just after assembly to lunch time. They were always supervised by the amiable Mr Uff. One such trip was to study the physical geography of the New Territories which was dominated by the mountain of Tai Mo Shan and the several rivers that flowed down from it – well when it rained anyway which was most summers except last summer when there was a drought and water rationing. On the subject of water the Hong Kong Government had decided to try and minimise the risk of shortages and rationing by building a new reservoir at a place called Plover Cove. Sited in the extreme north east of the New Territories the ambitious plan was to build a concrete dam across a bay which was roughly horse shoe shaped. Once completed the sea water contained therein would be pumped out completely and eventually replaced by fresh water caught in the run off from the territory's many hills and piped and pumped into the newly fresh water Plover Cove. It was a marvel of engineering in the making and was about half way to completion when our trip was made there. Copious notes were taken and sketches made in exercise books. Today it would be monosyllabic notes on an i-pad and instant pics with a few selfies thrown in for good measure no doubt.

I mentioned earlier that many thousands of refugees were rehoused in giant Resettlement Estates paid for by the Hong Kong Government. One such school trip took us to the Wong Tai Sin estate which was not too far from the school and the airport. A Chinese speaking guide took us round and we were free to speak to any of the residents as we took more notes for our books later. Every so often conversation would become impossible as a jet plane came in to land screaming over the rooftops. You can often see some of these in photos of 'old Hong Kong' where planes look as if they're going to land on someone's washing line. How very different it would all be if we were in UK. Where would school geography trips be to there? The North Yorkshire Moors maybe if we were lucky. At the time I don't think many of us realised just how fortunate we were to see the fag end of the British Empire turn into the richest city per capita in Asia right in front of our very eyes.

Spring turned into Summer. By the month of May the humidity was sky high again and thoughts turned back to swimming and sailing. By now we were all teenagers and we all became avid listeners of pop music. The most popular birthday presents of all were small transistor radios which you could hide in your school bag. The single wired earpiece was the only tell tale sign that Commercial Radio Hong Kong was blaring into your ear 'ole on the school bus or on the ferry. Many BBC radio presenters served their apprenticeships in Hong Kong including 'Stewpot' and Anneka Rice. My own little tranny was a Standard and Mike's was a Silver brand. The word tranny has a whole new meaning today of course and a small radio is not to be confused with a cross-dressing male.

I think the whole class was keen on pop music and to complement BBC's 'Pick of the Pops' we also had quite a lot of American pop music served up courtesy of Commercial Radio, Hong Kong. Motown, the combination of soul and pop, was the big thing and with half the Seventh Fleet seemingly in town at any given time the bars blared out the charms of Marvin Gaye's *'I heard it through the grapevine'* which was probably the biggest hit of 1968, in Hong Kong anyway. It was a golden year for pop on both sides of the Atlantic and in Britain the Beatles were going from strength to strength. Songs like 'Hey Jude' were popular choices for phone in requests and the dedications were sometimes so exhaustive as to be unreal:

'So this goes out from Ronnie Chan to all his friends at the Sacred Heart Connossian College – Judy Cho, Paul Chung, Venus Poon, Ursula Wong, Ricky Liu, Sonia Leung, Olive Wang, Vernon Lee, Veronique Kwok, Lisa Wu, Bert Chung (the tiring DJ starts playing the record as his voice weakens) Sally Lee, Martin Chu, Charles Wong, Victor Cho....and finally Napoleon Ng......it's *Born to be Wild* by Steppenwolf.....go for it baby!'

You get the drift. Repeat that twenty times per hour and that was Commercial Radio in Hong Kong in 1968. Like Marmite, you either loved or hated it.

Mike Davis came from a very musical family, his father Bob being a prominent tenor with the Robin Boyle Singers and his uncle a musician with the London Philharmonic. However, like his mate (me) he too was musically inept but we made up for it with periodic visits to a renowned record shop at the very top of Cat Street. More of a wide alley than a street the only access was by the vertical ascent of hundreds of steps that necessitated the agility of a goat and the oxygen capacity of a Tibetan yak. One Saturday morning we set off for the summit with several weeks savings from pocket money to buy the 'must have' LP of the day – Sergeant Pepper's Lonely Hearts Club Band by the Beatles. After many minutes of acute oxygen deprivation we arrived at the shop which really was more of a shack with a roof that leaked badly in heavy rain. I bought my copy immediately handing over the cost of HK$18 in notes and coins. Mike bought his too and we commenced our descent, I think to Queens Road. Mike, always the chap with an eye for a deal or a bargain waited until we were at street level, turned to me and said:

'Ha ha! I got mine for seventeen dollars. Ho Ho.' His mirth was short lived.

'Just check you bought the stereo version. They're always trying to palm you off with a mono at a dollar cheaper just to get rid of them.'

The look on Mike's face said it all and he resolved to go back another day to change it. Whether he actually did or not I don't know. However Mike also bought a single for his dad in the shape of 'Moon River' sung by the one and only Andy Williams. It was one of Bob's favourites and he too sung it beautifully. Specially written for the movie *Breakfast at Tiffanys* starring Audrey Hepburn whenever I hear it I think of dear Bob who left us over twenty years ago.

Looking back I guess music had quite an affect on our teenage lives and with electrical equipment from the likes of Sanyo, National Panasonic and Akai buyable at prices much cheaper than UK, many of us built up considerable record collections. Bob Dylan was in his heyday too, as was his British contemporary Donovan, and I probably bought half a dozen of their albums. Who can forget the haunting bars and lyrics of 'The Hurdy Gurdy Man?' or the foot tapping melody of 'Mellow Yellow' a not so oblique reference to a psychedelic drug?

1968 saw the birth, musically at least, of Jimi Hendrix and like him or not you had to admire his explosive talent. His double album Electric Ladyland was a major success in Hong Kong and was another one for Mike's collection.

Amazingly and despite the distractions of music and beaches I did quite well at the end of summer term exams and with the other 'favoured five' I sat my 'O' level maths with a paper each in Arithmetic, Algebra and Geometry. It would be a long wait for the results which were due out in late August. Fingers crossed.

At the end of term we said goodbye to some of our teachers who had completed their tours of duty, usually three years. They included Mr Uff our terrific Geography teacher who I was very sorry to see leave the school. His mantra of how to deal with crossing the International Date Line, in theory or practise, was the unforgettable 'As you go west a day goes west.' It was a year before I put it into practise myself when I crossed the Pacific on the s.s. *Orsova* but that is a story I have yet to tell. We also said goodbye to Miss Gilbert, our Deputy Head and my Chemistry teacher, a good one too. She was replaced as Deputy Head by the charming Miss McNeice, an Irish lady and a graduate of Queens University as I recall. She was also our new Geography teacher and would take us up to the 'O' level exam the following June. Following on from Mr Uff she inherited a very keen class indeed.

The last day of term was celebrated by lots of singing on the school bus of '*One man went to mow, went to mow a meadow*' and the ever popular '*The German Officer crossed the line, parlez vous?*' which proved beyond all doubt that the school language laboratory had been a sound investment.

For some obscure reason, I have no idea why, it was also a tradition to release hundreds of pieces of toilet paper, confetti style, from the windows of the school bus as it went through Repulse Bay. It was the old fashioned Izal paper and probably of more use as sandpaper than its intended function. Every single sheet was overprinted MOD PROPERTY so goodness knows what the residents of Repulse Bay made of this gesture.

On one particular last day of term unbeknown to all of us on the bus a car following behind was an Army car being driven by a uniformed Ghurkha with the rear seated passenger being a senior British officer. What happened after a particularly large expulsion of 'Izals' had landed on the car's windscreen and got caught up in the windscreen wipers was memorable. The Ghurkha was obviously ordered to overtake our bus which as we were now going uphill towards Chung Hom Kok was not difficult. Subsequent furious hand signals told us to slow and stop which our own driver did as he spotted the military insignia on the back of the Army car, probably a large Austin. Colonel Blimp got out of the car looking absolutely furious and made straight for the door of our bus and climbed aboard. He was livid and barked orders and commands left, right and centre.

'Disgraceful conduct! Absolutely disgraceful. You will all be on a charge tomorrow!'

How he could think that a bunch of civilian school kids could end up 'on a charge' I simply don't know but it was typical of pompous Army officers to think that anybody could be 'put on a charge.' He threatened that the Army would cease to provide a school bus at all if it happened again. Diplomatically the situation started to get totally out of hand when some stalwarts on the back row (usually the illicit smokers) started to sing again even before Blimp had got off:

'The *English* officer crossed the line, parlez-vous?' This sixth form inspired humour did not augur well for a good outcome. Sure enough a warning memo duly arrived at the desk of the CO at Little Sai Wan. I asked Dad what the outcome was.

'The CO has had a word with Arthur Jones, the bloke who runs our transport section. He says he'll lay on a bus if the Army back out. He says it's not a problem. Arthur doesn't like the Army.'

And so ended the summer term with six weeks of sun, beach, sailing and fishing ahead of us. Marvellous.

CHAPTER 14

One of the added advantages of being members of the Stanley Club was that it had access to its own beach which was called Tweed Bay. It was located a couple of hundred yards below the prison itself and at the end of a long winding path surrounded by quite lush vegetation. I was always wary of snakes on the path having seen one on more than one occasion even if they did skidaddle away at the first sensations of humans arriving. I recalled some warning notes about the McClelland's Coral snake that favoured terrain near to the coast and beaches, according to the Army memo anyway. All this was before Monty Python, so you took it seriously. The sandy beach was always pristine as any driftwood, rubbish or flotsam brought in from the South China Sea was removed by prisoners on daily 'beach cleaning' duty. There was apparently no shortage of volunteer prisoners to do this but I suppose that if you're a criminal who is banged up in a cell for most of the day then the opportunity to get some fresh air amid scenic surroundings was too good to miss. The waters too were usually crystal clear as there was no polluting industry or large human populations (excluding the prison) for miles. On good days the clarity of the water reminded me of Malta where it was like swimming in gin most of the time. The only exceptions were the days immediately following a typhoon or severe storm when strong winds whipped up the sand reducing visibility. About a hundred yards out from the shore a raft was positioned which was tethered to a stone anchor to stop it drifting. The depth of water was usually about twenty-five feet and we could manage to dive to the bottom and surface again exhaling like humpback whales as we resurfaced. Tweed Bay had been the site of some terrible atrocities perpetrated by the occupying Japanese against allied POWs with tales of prisoners being forced marched to the beach to bathe and then being machine gunned in the water. It is simply unimaginable today but in the Sixties many peoples' memories were still very raw. The Stanley Peninsular was the scene of bitter fighting against the invading Imperial Japanese Army in December 1941. That is outside the scope of this book, which is a personal memoir, but there are many good publications on the subject available today to which the internet affords almost immediate and affordable access.

Following in my father's footsteps I too learnt to play lawn bowls at the Stanley Club. In fact by that time there was a contingent of no less than four GCHQ chaps considered good enough to play in the league for the Club. Apart from Dad the others were the aforementioned Arthur Jones, Brian Cuthbert (Bazza's father) and one Chris Church who had the illustrious title of the 'Movements Officer' at Little Sai Wan. Let's hope he remembered to boil his water. Mr Church had actually been the official welcoming officer when we had arrived in the Colony on the *Bendoran* almost two years earlier. He was a big man with a large head and was known rather unflatteringly as 'Lurch.' He had a very odd delivery technique. Standing on the mat as normal, but just before bending and releasing the wood, he appeared to fall off the end of the mat as though someone had pushed him. He would end up two yards down the green before recovering his balance but by then the wood was well on its way. I guess that today somebody, probably the Club captain, would record him on a pocket sized camcorder and point out the unorthodoxy of his style. However it amused everyone who watched him but 'Lurch' was probably too busy concentrating to notice the green-side merriment. He and his wife Marion who had no children of their own, later adopted a Chinese girl from an orphanage. She was called Deirdre and everybody made a great fuss of her.

Apart from several 'hangmen' there were some real characters amongst the first team's members. There was B. Singh of course, always telling everybody to 'be up' and an Aussie called Bruce Denham who worked in the Commercial Department of the Australian High Commission. Although slight of frame with legs like sparrows he also played Number Three and his penetrative voice carried a long way. He was a brilliant player too.

The green itself was well tended at the Stanley Club – just as you might expect with free prison labour on hand to roll it in between match days. The roller was immense, about six feet wide and needed six prisoners (three at each end) to manoeuvre it successfully up and down the green hundreds of times whatever the temperature, usually about thirty three Celsius in the summer months. The drum of the roller was hollow and could be filled with water to increase its effectiveness. It was almost certainly the only bowling green in the world to be tended by prison labour.

On match days the dozen selected team members would meet in the Club bar at about one 'o' clock for a liquid team talk and multiple imbibings of San Miguel. Play didn't start until three 'o' clock in the hope that the sun was past its fiercest but this also had its downside. As soon as the sun started to set, darkness followed quickly, as it does in the Tropics. Many a match was finished off by a Number Three holding a lit Zippo lighter over the jack to show the Skip the way in. Other teams in Division Three particularly liked playing 'away' at the Stanley Club with its shaded verandah, Flame of the Forest trees and open views to the sea and the sky. Many of the Clubs, particularly those in Kowloon, were just tiny green oases surrounded by tall buildings and noisy traffic and by comparison the Stanley Club must have appeared as a Garden of Eden.

And on that topic, and to revert to music, there was one particular charts hit (in Hong Kong anyway) that blew my mind away. It was called *'In a Gadda da Vida'* played by an American band called the Iron Butterfly. Recorded on Long Island, New York in June 1968 it was a totally new and sensational sound. Legend had it that the producer was either high or drunk when he listed the title and that he had meant to call it In a Garden of Eden. We will never know. The full length version is seventeen minutes long but it was normally the abridged seven minute version that was played on Commercial Radio.

The summer of '68 was joyful with the Club, Stanley Beach, St Stephens Beach and the Army Yacht Club all within easy reach. With Class C helmsman certificates under our belt Bazza and I asked if we could take an Enterprise out for half a day. The Welch Regiment was soon going to be rotated and replaced with another so to be honest they probably didn't give a fig if we brought the boat back in one piece or not. Armed with cheese sandwiches, Coke and more than a few San Migs we set off south to see if could reach the distant islands to the south when we would 'ready about lee ho' and come home. We probably got about two miles before a HK Marine Police launch appeared out of nowhere and an English voice boomed through a hand held megaphone:

'Where the hell do you two think you're going?' One of us pointed south towards the Dan Gan Islands. 'Oh no you're bloody not. They're Communist not ours. Where have you come from?'

We told him we were from St. Stephens Army Yacht Club and the boat was borrowed with permission. Suddenly a rope was thrown by a Chinese crew member which landed bang in the centre of the boat. The megaphone boomed again 'Tie this to the bloody front end, lower your mainsail and hang on tight.'

It was definitely the only time I travelled at about twenty knots in a sailing boat. We were soon back at the Yacht Club to the amazement of the watching Taffies. We were tempted to say that the weather had been quite nice in Dan Gan but we thought better of it. Probably just as well.

It was a particularly hot summer even by Hong Kong standards with the mercury touching 34/35 Celsius, sometimes for days on end. Out of the blue one day, and probably out of holiday boredom, Steve Ryan suggested that we two walked from Stanley to Little Sai Wan, a distance of about seven miles. I was up for it. Liberally splashed with sun cream (we were both fair skinned) we set off about 11 'o' clock and hoped to reach Sai Wan by about 1pm. The first two miles was on the level and took us to the dam at Tai Tam Reservoir. Boy was it hot, even hotter than normal and we could see the tarmac on the road surface visibly melting. The Number 14 Bus from Shau Ki Wan had left its tracks on the dam. We were wearing trainers, or plimsolls as we called them then before they became trendy and expensive. Our feet stuck to the surface as we crossed the dam like we were treading on chewing gum. It got hotter and hotter and we were grateful for the several bottles of drinks we carried with us. It was Coke, 7UP or Green Spot in those days, no fancy mineral waters or so called energy drinks at a dollar a mouthful. Another two miles uphill and we reached the junction for Shek O, Big Wave Bay and ultimately Sai Wan which, fortuitously, was now downhill although still another three miles distant. I had never known it be so hot. An hour later we were on the verandah of Ariel House drinking more Coke and consuming Club sandwiches for which Ariel House had a wonderful reputation. I bumped into my Dad who was on his lunch break. He was amazed.

'You've walked?! What from Stanley?! Do you know how hot it is today?'

The next day's papers were full of 'Hot stories' mostly about traffic accidents caused by melting roads but another one caught my eye. It was from the head of the Marine Department at Hong Kong University who had warned that above normal temperatures had almost certainly been the reason why a large school of tiger sharks had swum close in to the shore at Repulse Bay. Maybe they were just following schools of smaller fish for lunch as it were. Either way it caused a temporary blip in the swimming habits of Repulse Bay residents for a few days and Alouette helicopters from the Royal Hong Kong Auxiliary Air Force went out shark spotting around the beaches for a few days. Sharks were never considered to be a real problem in Hong Kong waters but there were sightings from time to time and every public beach had a 'watch tower' with a chap with binoculars and a bell to ring if he was awake and spotted anything nasty in the water. However, sadly I think there were two fatalities during the three years I was there and both involved people from the fishing community swimming from junks out in

Mirs Bay. The magnitude of fatalities amongst escaping refugees swimming to freedom would never be known. Towards the end of the school holiday Steve and I repeated the exercise but on a cooler day – probably about 32C. No problem.

CHAPTER 15

In that month of August though we did finally get a "bulls eye" hit by a full blooded typhoon. She was called Shirley. We always studied the weather report and what they called the General Situation over China, the South China Sea and the western Pacific. The circular areas labelled 'LOW' surrounded by isobars were the first tell tale signs that a 'tai-fung' might be about to form. Very often they were still over a thousand miles away but still you watched them like a hawk. So, fortunately, did Uncle Sam's Navy.

Slowly but surely in about the middle of that month, the 'LOW' in the western Pacific developed into a proper Tropical Depression and assumed the structure and pattern of a cyclone. This means strong winds start to move in anti-clockwise circles around an 'Eye' where the barometric pressure just keeps dropping. This Depression moved slowly westwards towards the main Philippine island of Luzon. As it intensified it was formally named Shirley by the International Weather Bureau. This naming procedure was to distinguish it from other cyclones that might have already developed or were 'on the way' so to speak. For the next day Shirley continued to move west and clipped the northern tip of Luzon which probably slowed down its speed, at least for a short while. Very soon it was in the

South China Sea proper so to speak and altered its course to west north west. At this point the Royal Observatory started to take a closer look and it released a satellite picture to TV channels and newspapers. Crossing Pratas Reef the threat to Hong Kong started to look very real and Typhoon Signal Number One was hoisted. At this point thousands of small vulnerable boats headed for the many typhoon shelters around the Colony.

Later that same day the Signal was increased to Number Three as winds started to freshen. Shirley altered course again taking a more north-westerly course and for the first time in many years it looked as if a direct hit was possible. In fact records showed that an 'Eye' had only passed over the Royal Observatory once since the War, in 1961 to be precise. The culprit in that case was, I believe, Typhoon Wanda. Mindful of the destruction Wanda had caused seven years earlier bigger vessels that were able to put to sea to ride out the storm. Winds gusted to fifty knots and Signal number seven was hoisted. Weather stations at Waglan Island and Taits Cairn were starting to report gusts of over seventy knots and it was quite obvious that Hong Kong was in for a battering.

The caretaker, Ah-Hoy, came round every flat with huge rolls of sticky brown tape like masking tape with instructions to stick it 'criss cross fashion' over all our main windows. In the event of windows shattering this would hopefully prevent shards of glass showering like bullets all over the flat. It was starting to get quite scary even for us in a secure concrete building. What must it have felt like for a family huddling in a hut on a hillside?

One of our fellow families in Gordon Terrace did have a major problem. Tom and Doreen Cass were expecting their third baby any day now to add to their two daughters

Dorinda and Rowena. We were relieved to see an Army ambulance arrive to take her to BMH, the British Military Hospital in Kowloon. Presumably they managed to catch a vehicular ferry before they stopped running altogether which was now a virtual certainty. There was no cross harbour tunnel in those days. We just hoped they were going to make it on time.

Our cable TV packed up which was a sure sign that things were not going well. We all stuck like glue to the radio and the bulletins issued by the Royal Observatory. It was dark, the rain was torrential, the lights were flickering and worse still the glass in the windows visibly started to bend inwards. If they shattered we just hoped that the tape would do its job. The metal casing on the street lamp in the centre of the roundabout was only about a hundred feet away and started to wobble. If it snapped off then a mega-gust could propel it like a cannonball straight towards our window. It could be lethal. Dad watched it like a hawk.

Number Ten signal, the highest one of all, was hoisted late in the evening. Then suddenly it all went very, very quiet. This meant that the 'Eye' was passing directly over us. We had omitted one thing in our preparations. We had forgotten to bring the rattan and metal balcony furniture inside the flat. Measuring the diameter of the 'Eye' and therefore the lull in the storm was not a precise science. It could be ten minutes or an hour. We didn't take any chances as Dad and I unsecured the balcony doors and brought all the balcony furniture inside rapido. It was an eerie stillness outside and quite unforgettable. There wasn't even the whisper of any wind and bizarrely other folk were out on their balconies too just chatting, perhaps over a fag and a coffee.

Then, without warning, it was back. Whammo. The wind whipped up from the opposite direction to that previously as the 'Eye' had passed over. The north easterly barrage now came from the south-west straight towards us. The Royal Observatory reported gusts at between one hundred and one hundred and ten knots. Add ten percent to miles per hour and that becomes very scary indeed. Dad looked again for the lamp, this time with binoculars through the darkness and almost horizontal rain. It had gone! Where was it?

In all the fright we had, regrettably, forgotten all about poor Doreen Cass. Had the baby arrived and if it was a girl then surely they would call her Shirley? The girl would be able to dine out on that one all her life. Nobody had any news it seemed.

Typhoon Shirley maintained her course and moved inland into Kwantung Province. Solid land is bad news for typhoons as there is no warm air coming off a warm sea to maintain the toxic mix of wind and low pressure. The storm slowly dissipated, Shirley was downgraded once again to the status of Tropical Storm and the Signals reduced accordingly. By morning it was time to assess the damage. Fortunately we had no windows broken, just the irritating job of removing all the sticky tape with hot soapy water. I think the flats on the top floor suffered some water ingress from the roof and guess what they found on the roof? Yes, the lamp from the street light, minus the glass of course. I do not recall any fatalities on land or at sea, so expert had the Royal Observatory become in its forecasting. With a little help from a satellite and Uncle Sam's Navy of course. We were all so very relieved and slowly but surely life returned to normal even if it did rain a lot for several days.

A few days later Mrs Doreen Cass returned from BMH with her new born baby girl. They named her Georgina.

Bang went all those free dinners at the stroke of a pen on a birth certificate.

CHAPTER 16

After 'Shirley' life became a little dull by comparison but we still had a couple of weeks left before returning to St Georges for the Autumn term and we sure made the most of it. Dad still got his annual leave allowance even though we were eight thousand miles from home. But where exactly was home? Service and GCHQ families spent many years overseas in many different territories and to many the distinction between 'home' and 'abroad' had become blurred. Either way the notion of holidays to the UK to see friends and family was a complete 'no no' in those days. The cost was simply prohibitive. A BOAC or PanAm return ticket in the Sixties cost over five hundred pounds, a fortune by comparison with the plethora of cheap online fares available today. The age of the Jumbo jet, which revolutionised passenger plane economics, had yet to dawn.

So we contented ourselves with outings, drives and excursions to parts of the Colony we had visited either seldom or not at all. We would have liked to go to Macau some forty miles west on the other side of the Pearl delta but it was still 'off limits' for security reasons. So the furthest you could actually travel was the Island of Lantau. At three times the area of Hong Kong Island it was the biggest in the Territory, mountainous and sparsely populated. We had heard quite a bit about it from some of the Prison officers at the Stanley Club as there was a small, low security prison on Lantau called Chi Ma Wan on the east of the island. One of the officers, called John Millbank, spent quite a lot of time at Chi Ma Wan and had passed some tips on to Dad – where to go, how to get there, what to see, what to avoid.

So one hot day towards the end of August we drove the Cortina into town and parked at the Star Ferry. The Outlying Islands ferry terminal was about five minutes walk away and a rudimentary timetable was chalked up on a board. No electronic displays in those days. The ferry would take us to Silver Mine Bay, then Lantau's largest settlement and mostly comprising fisherfolk, via another tiny island called Peng Chau. The ferry was for foot passengers only. Bigger vehicular ferries only took cars to Lantau at much less frequent intervals. Whether John Millbank had advised Dad not to take the car or not I don't know but we found out later that it had been a wise choice. Leaving central Hong Kong and heading towards the western approaches gave a terrific view of the scale of the growth of the urbanised area. Even in the late Sixties the area known as Western District had swelled into another called Kennedy Town which was the end of the line for the trams. Pok Fu Lam (which of course we all called 'Pok Fulham') was a new township just slightly further around the island contours but it was only a matter of time before it would form just one vast expanse of urban sprawl.

I think it took about an hour to get to Silver Mine Bay and we saw lots of shipping including a huge American carrier at anchor that was probably too big to sail into the inner harbour in safety. Next day's papers revealed it to to be none other than the 'Big E' or more correctly the *USS Enterprise* (the carrier not the starship) one of the earliest nuclear powered warships. She would not be the only nuclear vessel to visit Hong Kong that year.

Although cold drinks had been available on the ferry it was very hot so we soon found an open air café with chilled San Mig for Dad and Coke for the rest of us. We had a walk around the quite large bay that had a public pier as well as the berths for the ferries. Two small but interesting vessels were berthed along side. One was obviously a 'fire tender' with huge water cannons facing fore and aft like guns on a destroyer. It was called the *Alexander Grantham* and was very impressive in her red livery. She looked quite sleek and modern. The other, smaller, vessel was reminiscent of a bygone age. With a tall single funnel amidships she looked like something you might have seen in *African Queen* or sailing on Windermere with Beatrix Potter taking afternoon tea on the quarterdeck. I stared at her for ages which is probably why the name on her stern stayed with me. She was called *Sir Cecil Clementi* which at the time struck me as bizarre. With a name like that shouldn't she be sailing on Lake Como or Lake Garda in northern Italy? It would be many years before I discovered the origin of both vessels' names.

There was some repair and remedial work going on at the pier involving some new concreting and, lo and behold, some manual work involving a heavy roller with six men puffing and blowing in the hot sun. A man who looked like a supervisor was sat on a nearby wall barking out orders. It was just like the bowling green at the Stanley Club. The penny suddenly dropped with Dad.

'Of course, these guys are prisoners too. I'll bet they're from Chi Ma Wan.'

Dad chatted briefly to the man on the wall who was a Chinese prison officer and spoke good English. They shared a fag and when the officer still had about three drags left on his he threw it towards the prisoners. The handles on the roller were immediately dropped as they all raced towards the still smouldering fag on the ground. Can you imagine that? As we walked towards an open air café for a spot of lunch Dad looked over his shoulder, whistled towards the prisoners and threw his pack of Rothman's behind him. All hell broke loose as all six raced to be the first to grab it. Goodness knows what the warden thought. I often wondered if he gave them a light.

Lunch was memorable and consisted of steamed prawns and then more steamed prawns. They were simply huge, like small bananas. You bought them by weight called a katty which I think was about a pound and a half in Imperial measurements. That was the uncooked weight so I guess that by the time the shells, legs, tails and alimentary canals had been removed the net edible weight was about a pound. The last anatomical item had to be gotten rid of as prawns, being bottom feeders, could give you a nasty dose of the 'squits' if you were not careful. They were so delicious we ordered another half a katty.

On John Millbank's recommendation we got on a 'Pak Pie' similar to those that ran in the New Territories. I think there were only two different destinations to choose from and we were headed for Shek Pik and a Buddhist Monastery at or near the summit of a very high hill that was best described as a small mountain. The small bus that probably seated about a dozen people legally, was crammed with about twice that number of human beings and ten times that number of live chickens in wire cages. We were all sat near the back which was a big mistake. To say that Lantau roads were not good was a gross understatement and sitting at the rear simply magnified the bounce effect. We all felt a bit green. The road followed the coast roughly south-west and the beach seemed to go on for miles. Eventually the road turned right and started to go uphill. The engine groaned under pressure from the load and gradient. This was definitely not Bob Davis's Zodiac going up Tai Mo Shan. It got markedly cooler as we gained altitude and soon we found ourselves looking down on our left to a large reservoir. Twelve months earlier, during the drought, it had been almost empty. Today it was full to the brim. We were relieved to reach the Po Lin Monastery and got off the bus. We were offered soft drinks and refreshments courtesy of the resident monks all dressed in the traditional saffron robes and me being, a big Donovan fan, I started humming:

'I'm just mad about saffron...they call me Mellow Yellow....yeah...'

This brought forth a penetrating elbow in the ribs from a not amused father. We were offered a look around inside and rang bells. Lots of presumably novice monks were sat on their haunches humming and muttering incantations. I have no idea what it was but it wasn't Mellow Yellow that's for sure. After a half an hour or so we bade our farewells, made a donation to Buddha on a proffered dish and waited for the next Pak Pie to take us back to Silver Mine Bay. The descent to sea level was even hairier as going downhill made you even more aware of the gradient and the inherent danger if the brakes failed. Accidents, and fatalities, were frequent and it was with relief when we were at beach level, this time with the South China Sea on our right, as we sped back to the ferry terminal. The fire tender had departed but *Sir Cecil Clementi* was still there waiting presumably for Beatrix and Peter the Rabbit to board. It was dark by the time we got home to Stanley. It was our first and last family outing to Lantau.

Another 'one off' family trip we did that year was to Stonecutters Island. Situated about a mile due west of central Kowloon it was operated entirely by the Forces, indeed civilians were barred from it at all times, it being used as a munitions dump I believe. However it did have one very nice advantage – a large salt water swimming pool that was usually very quiet as you might expect due to its isolation. A colleague of Dad's who lived in Kowloon, a jovial Liverpudlian called Frank Rees, went there regularly with his lovely Northern Irish wife, Flo, and their two daughters, Yvonne and Valerie. 'Would we all like to join them one day?' You betcha. Arrangements were made.

We drove to Star ferry and went across the harbour to Kowloon side. Adjacent to the famous clock tower, which was one of the first landmarks that 'Squirrel' Hatton had pointed out to me two years earlier, were some 'Steps' this being the euphemism for where boats could tie up. We met up with the Rees family and before very long a Royal Navy tender appeared alongside with a makeshift gangplank lowered from its deck-side to the concrete steps. There was a bit of a swell and Mum was not looking forward to the transfer from terra firma to what was perhaps the smallest of Britannia's vessels East of Suez. Eventually we were all safely on board and the boat headed off around the huge Ocean Terminal out into more open waters and Stonecutters Island ahead of us. It was a glorious day and a great time was had by all. Today, Stonecutters exists as a promontory of West Kowloon and is no longer an island. A far sighted British Government ensured that when HMS Tamar was closed in the run up to the Handover, its replacement was built on Stonecutters. Nobody wanted a communist PLA Navy base in the centre of town a stone's throw from the stock exchange.

That was the first of several outings and social events we shared with the lovely Rees family. In reciprocation we took them all to Tweed Bay one day followed by tea at Gordon Terrace. Coming from Liverpool and being a natural Beatles fan, Frank amazed us all by singing along with all the lyrics to Eleanor Rigby when it came on the radio during our meal. Once a scouser, always a scouser I guess. Decades later, I was very touched at Frank's funeral when one of his grandsons delivered the eulogy and described a day out with his grandfather in his last days. It was he said, 'just a perfect day' and immediately I thought back to our day on Stonecutters Island. That too had been a 'perfect day.'

Sometime that summer we also said goodbye to the Simpson family from Gordon Terrace. Not Homer & Co. but Ivor, his wife Freda and son Ian. They left Hong Kong on the P & O Liner *Canberra* and we were invited on board for drinks in the now customary manner before she sailed. We could not possibly have foreseen that years later the whole world would watch her on TV as she transported British troops to the Falkland Islands following the invasion by Argentina.

Two more notable events happened before we went back to school. The 1st Battalion the Duke of Wellington's Regiment replaced the Welch Regiment in garrison at Stanley Fort. The second was that I received a letter from the school telling me that I had achieved a Grade C Pass in my maths O level. Like Mafeking, I was relieved. I could now bin Maths and concentrate on the other subjects. Or at least that's what I thought anyway.

CHAPTER 17

'So you see, Mark, there is no reason why you can't now continue with what is called Additional Maths.' So said a well meaning but mistaken adviser at St. Georges.

Yeah right, that was a violation of the Trades Description Act if ever there was one. Adding and subtracting had absolutely nothing to do with it. Welcome to the mysterious world of Calculus. Normal maths was nearly all figures with just the odd letter or two such as: In a Pythagoras triangle, Angle A is 35° so what is Angle B? etc. But when you take out all the figures to leave just letters, most of them resembling Greek ones to boot like Epsilon or Omega (which I always thought was a watch) then normal maths logic just flies out of the window. To mortal folk, like me, this creates a big problem. I very quickly reached the conclusion that Calculus was the most useless branch of mathematics ever invented. Unwisely I pursued it all the remaining year at St. Georges. Big mistake. My time would have been better spent learning the breeding habits of the Portuguese Man of War, a particularly nasty jellyfish that invaded Hong Kong's beaches at certain times of the year.

As usual as old pals left so new pupils joined us in Class 5A in the shape of one Ben Cromarty and one Christopher Edge, from Army and Navy families respectively. Benjie, as he preferred to be called was bilingual in English and Flemish, his mother being Belgian. Benjie was a star at everything he studied and was the natural replacement for the cranial Cliff Dive as the class brainbox. Chris Edge was a chirpy, down to earth chappie who lived at the Navy flats at Harcourt Place in Happy Valley. He would replace me as 'top of the class' at Geography but I forgave him.

Like maths, English was going from bad to even worse. Literature involved studying Chaucer for the first time. I ask you, reading Chaucer in the most vibrant city on earth? What a farce. I would far sooner read the South China Morning Post. Although widely regarded as the greatest English poet of the Middle Ages and the winner of Britain's Got Talent in 1380, this man was the bane of my life. The main book we had to study was about a cockerel called Chanticleer and his mate, a hen called Pertelote. It is a sad reflection on the level of brainwashing that I had to endure in the autumn of 1968 that I can actually remember the names of those damn chickens. They should have become Vindaloo and Madras before the end of the 14th century but for the fact that the British Empire had not moved east by then. It was simply brain numbing and an affront to anyone with an IQ above ten This torture went on for weeks. In fact it got worse with the addition of Shakespeare's Henry the Fourth Part One. Or was it Two? I can only remember one single line from the whole miserable book spoken by some bloke called Gaunt:

'I wasted time and now doth time waste me!'

To right and too much time. To this day I take the view that the only lines of the Bard worth remembering are from Richard the Second and end with the words:

'This blessed plot, this earth, this realm, this England.'

Geography, my best and favourite subject, was still going well and Miss McNeice proved a very capable replacement for Mr Uff. In the run up to O level the following June we still had the whole of the British Isles to cover. She was stunned however to discover that nearly all of us were ignorant of UK geography to an almost calamitous level. One day she handed out photocopies (yes they had just come in) of a blank map of the UK. We had to put numbers on the map to geographically locate towns, cities, rivers etc. For example, No. 1 Bristol No. 2 Belfast No.3 The Forth Bridge No.4 The River Thames and so on. You get the general drift.

On checking the papers once handed in Miss McNeice had a nasty shock with Bristol turning up in Wales, Belfast in Kent and other howlers. However when she asked everyone in turn where they had lived for the last few years and the majority of answers ranged from Singapore to Libya to West Germany then she came to understand the magnitude of the task in front of her. Most of us were worldly wise but UK ignorant. She set upon the task with alacrity and by Christmas we were all UK savvy. There were no more 'Uff style' field trips until the following July and details of that will blow your mind later.

From my viewpoint 1968 had been a very good year for 'ship spotting' and it was a good job I was not a 'train spotter' too as the KCR only owned (I think) six Australian built diesel locomotives numbered, strangely, from 51 to 56. Why they were not numbered from 1 to 6 I cannot tell you but that's life. Maybe numbers 1 to 50 are still chugging around mines and cattle stations in backwater New South Wales. You just never know in Australia.

Back to ships. I had been aboard *Canberra*, as I have mentioned, and I had seen her before in Grand Harbour, Valletta on her maiden voyage to Australia. The newly completed flyover alongside HMS Tamar now afforded us a bird's eye view of the naval basin and all visiting British and

Commonwealth ships. US ships were always at anchor in the harbour, never tied up alongside, for some reason. That end of summer *Hermes* had been again and was berthed on Tamar's North Wall in full view. We actually looked down on the flight deck from the height of the bus on the flyover. One of her Sea Vixen fighter planes had had a prang with a heavy landing and was badly damaged. Newspapers showed a picture of the bent plane being craned off and reloaded onto the deck of the s.s. *Benarty* a sister ship of *Bendoran* which is why I remembered it so clearly. *Benarty* was specially equipped with new Stulcken cranes that could easily lift the twenty tons and more of the stricken Vixen. If only Chanticleer and Pertelote had fallen victim to a vixen in the 14th century I might have been spared hours of mental torture.

We were also visited that year by the Australian aircraft carrier HMAS *Melbourne,* designed and built for the Royal Navy as the *Majestic* but adapted for the RAN and then sold. In service for almost three decades she was the supreme example of what a light carrier can achieve at tremendous value for money to the Australian tax-payer. This was a lesson totally lost on the Europe obsessed sea blind goons that professed to run Britain between 1964 and 1997. Only now in the second decade of the 21st century is Britain re-learning the value of carrier power.

Perhaps the most interesting ship I saw that year was one I spotted at the Ocean Terminal with no funnel. It looked very odd indeed but the mystery was solved in a newspaper which revealed that it was the nuclear powered NS (nuclear ship) *Savannah*, an American freighter. Ordered and financed by Eisenhower's 'Atoms for Peace Program' in the late Fifties she was built to show that atomic physics could be useful in civilian life as well as for military purposes.

With the sole exception of Russian nuclear powered ice-breakers she was the only civilian nuclear ship in the world. Commercially however she was doomed to be a failure. You just could not possibly imagine the canny Jocks that owned the Ben Line forking out squillions for *Savannahs* when they could buy their *Benlomonds* for a fraction of that on the Clyde. Fifty years later there are no nuclear freighters anywhere in the world and the *Savannah* is a de-fuelled museum exhibit in Baltimore, Maryland. Mind you there's no more ships built on the Clyde either so where does that leave us?

Back in Stanley the new soldiers were settling in well, had taken over the Yacht Club with mixed success and the 'Shack' in the village with total success. They were obviously adapting well from their native Yorkshire Tetleys Bitter to local San Miguel and fights and disturbances with the locals were fairly minimal and usually restricted to Saturday night when the beer money ran out. If the Doors version of 'Light my Fire' was played much more on the juke box the needle would soon wear through and start playing the flip side. On the school bus that ran straight from Stanley Fort ' One Man went to Mow' was soon replaced by 'On Ilkley Moor Bar Tat' which probably caused the Chinese drivers to wonder just what planet they came from. Having lived in Yorkshire myself I knew only too well.

There was however a local festival during that term and it was called, appropriately, the Mid Autumn Festival. It is essentially the Chinese equivalent of the Harvest Festival widely celebrated in Christian Europe and is often referred to as the Harvest Moon Festival. It is traditional to eat 'mooncakes' and to offer them to friends, family and business associates. The cakes themselves are what most Europeans would call a sticky bun about five inches in diameter and about an inch thick. Filled usually with lotus seed paste they are very sweet and 'moreish' as we might say. The island of Cheung Chau, south east of Lantau, had its own unique way of celebrating with a tall tower made entirely of bamboo which was covered in mooncakes. There was always a race to see who could clamber the tower the quickest to acquire the mooncakes at the very top. Longevity was guaranteed for the winners. Indeed the Chinese character or symbol for longevity was traditionally marked on the top of every mooncake and in this respect it was not dissimilar to a 'x' on a hot cross bun at Easter.

It was easy for us Westerners to empathise with the Harvest Moon Festival but perhaps less so with the annual festival of Ching Ming or the Tomb Sweeping Festival. Taking place (in Hong Kong at least) on either the fourth of fifth day of April it is the day when traditionally families descend on hillside cemeteries to 'sweep and clean' the graves of their ancestors. Indeed it is often referred to as 'Ancestors' Day. Faux money and other paper images of wealth are burnt at the graveside to provide deceased family members with assets in the afterlife. Offerings of food, especially fruit, would also be made and the whole event took on more the mantra of a picnic than an act of commemoration but that is through my eyes, not a Chinese person's. There is no doubt that Chinese respect their ancestors to a much higher level than we Westerners and they venerate age that in some ways makes us appear almost mockingly dismissive of the elderly. Many years later in the Eighties, Premier Deng Xiaoping was asked by a Western journalist why all the members of the Chinese Politburo were in their eighties. His reply was almost immediate:

'Because all the ninety year olds are dead.' You see what I mean.

Other festivals such as 'Tin Hau' who was the Goddess of the Seas and the now almost ubiquitous Dragon Boat Festival were were enjoyed by locals and expatriates alike, the latter being Hong Kong's equivalent of the Henley Regatta. Competition was fierce between teams that represented schools, villages and companies and races took place all over the Colony. Today, dragon boat races are common the world over but it all started in Southern China. I have digressed awhile on these festivals and customs but it is important to remember that although we followed our own Western holidays we were immersed in a culture far older than our own.

With the end of the Autumn term Christmas, our last one in Hong Kong, was soon in sight. The plastic artificial Christmas tree that we had bought at the Stanley Fort NAAFI for HK$66 dollars (I remember that because it coincided with the actual year of '66) was brought out of its box and reassembled from the hundred plus individual branches, stems, fronds and needles. Plus, of course, the lights. It was always the lights that were the problem. In the days before wiring was done in parallel instead of in series, if one bulb went duff then the whole show stopped. Each bulb then had to be screwed out and individually tested with a torch battery to establish which one was the culprit. It caused more rows than anything and I would like to nominate the inventor of 'parallel wired Christmas tree lights' for a Nobel Peace Prize. Today of course that sort of nonsense is won only by failed politicians so there are plenty of nominees without me throwing my ha'porth in. Dad was 'Father Christmas' again at the Salesian School in Shau Ki Wan and it would be for the last time. It was our last 'warm' Christmas and the thought of a 'cold' Christmas next year was simply awful.

CHAPTER 18

Christmas 1968 was notable for the people who weren't there as many of our friends and neighbours had left back for the UK. This included the Simpsons who were always generous hosts on the day itself. I spent at least some of the school holiday preparing for the 'mock' O levels to be held in January, not to mention the real O level English Language in the same month. I did no work or revision for English Literature whatsoever having had my fill of Gaunt and medieval chickens.

The day of the English Language examination arrived and we all had butterflies in our stomachs. I always found the opening words of the invigilator quite chilling, I'm not sure why.

'Be careful to read the questions properly. Do not answer any more questions than you are asked. You may now turn over the papers and commence. You have three hours.'

You would have thought that they might at least have said 'Good luck' or even 'Good joss' but even staff that you thought you knew quite well morphed into demons and vigilantes on exam days. I turned over the paper and went straight to the essay section:

'Choose ONE of the following titles and write an essay of approximately five hundred words.'

As if you would do more than one! I looked down the list of options. It reminded me of looking down the list of titles on the front cover of the Readers Digest and as your eyes moved south you either immediately discarded them or kept them in mind for possible future reading. The choice was simply dreadful and my heart sank. The penultimate choice was 'Music and Man' and I thought that maybe, just maybe, I could make a fist of that one but......and then.... salvation...'The Storm.'

With memories of Typhoon Shirley still fresh in my mind this was manna from heaven. If, somewhere in the world, my exam papers still exist and were not shredded then what you read in Chapter 15 was what I wrote, almost verbatim, for my essay. I cannot remember a single thing about the rest of the exam.

The mock O levels on all the other subjects went well with the sole exception of English Literature which was, as expected, a disaster verging on the literary equivalent of Pompeii. The French oral exam went especially well I thought and I enunciated my vowels in true 'allo 'allo fashion. All we had to do now was wait for the results. The English Language exam was external so it would be a good few weeks before any news there but the internal ones soon brought forth either joy or damnation. I received both.

'And this,' Harland, 'is the most disgraceful paper I have seen. I have saved it till last. I will read some of it to the class. Gaunt...blah blah blah...I have never had anyone quote Shakespeare in a Chaucer essay. 3% just disgraceful.'

I thought he was going to have a fit so I didn't say anything at all, just staying schtum. Poor bloke. The rest of my results were fair to good and I got an 'A' for French! I was excused from all further English lessons (phew) on condition that I had passed the O level Language exam when the results arrived from London the following month. I did. Hooray! Three cheers for Typhoon Shirley -hip hip.. but seriously it was time to start doing some serious work and revision with four more O levels in French, Geography, Physics and Chemistry only three months away.

It was after these 'mocks' that we had a short academic break as it were. An Orienteering competition was organised which had replaced the cross country runs due to snakes and trains. We were separated into two groups – marshals and runners. I opted for the former having taken the view a long time ago that running was reserved for four legged members of the 'kingdom animalia.' The boat building instructor, Davies, was the chief architect of this latest exercise in athletic futility. Marshals were to be in pairs which alone gave you warning that this was not going to be a walk in the park. Likewise the runners were in pairs. My 'oppo' as a marshal was Benjie and on the day we received our joining instructions. Yes, more of the damn things. We were given a map of northern Kowloon and were horrified to see that our marshalling station was at the top of Lion Rock. They had to be joking. Although only about a mile due north of St. Georges it would take us well over an hour to get there on foot and ascend to the cross marked on the map.

We ran out of roads and then paths and started to climb. Vegetation gave way to scrub and then finally just a face of crumbling rock. The angle of dangle got steeper as the view behind us started to take on that of a hawk. We were not amused but constant checking with the map assured us that we were heading in the right direction. It got steeper and steeper not to mention very slippery. The decomposed granite was just like sand after Hong Kong's bone dry winter. Eventually we reached some sort of a minor plateau and decided to 'make camp' as it were. The next escarpment above us was probably another thirty to forty feet higher and neither of us felt very comfortable at the thought of climbing further. I had taken my Standard transistor radio and we settled down to sandwiches and drinks that we had brought with us. It was probably about twelve noon and we figured we were well in time before the first runners would start coming through. The view was amazing as we looked down on Kai Tak airport and the jet liners swooping in low towards the red and white checkerboard that was their marker to turn sharp right before flopping down onto the concrete ribbon beyond the traffic filled roundabout. At this height and without the noise of the jet engines it was most peaceful and the planes might as well have been gliders. Half way through our sandwiches our solace was suddenly rudely interrupted by a horrendous noise.

Do you remember the TV series *Mash* set in the Korean War? Unbelievably screaming up the mountainside towards us was an Army Bell helicopter – one of those with a huge glass cockpit to give the pilot and observer maximum view. It drew level with us and hovered about a hundred feet away and the pilot turned the fuselage so that the observer was facing straight at us. Wearing a helmet, sunglasses and brandishing a portable loud-hailer it was Davies, the boat builder turned aviator.

'Go higher, I want you two higher, another twenty feet, higher!'

I looked at Benjie, he looked at me. This wasn't good. Chopper Davies was not going away and the Bell continued to hover. We packed our bags and started to move higher up and the Bell went into a swallow dive towards Kai Tak.

'I think this is far enough, sod Davies.'

'Agreed. It will take the runners ages to get up here to get their logbooks stamped. We'll stay about half way up this last bit.'

An hour later the runners started to come through. They were not amused at the last almost vertical bit of the climb so we spared them all the trouble. The log books were chucked up to us the last twenty or so feet, stamped and thrown back. Mike and his running mate were two of the first runners through but on a future occasion he would prefer two wheels to two legs as you will discover. I can't remember who won. Who cares? At least the view was nice.

I did however have one weekend's break with no school work at all. It was March 1st, St. David's Day and a Saturday. I don't know whose idea it originally was and apologies all round if it was mine. Six of us blokes from school decided to walk right around Hong Kong Island, clockwise, from Stanley to Stanley. We didn't know exactly how far it was in road miles but we thought no less than twenty five. We must have been absolutely bonkers. The six were myself, Ben Cromarty, Andrew Barnett, Geoffrey Bryant, Steve Ryan and Mike Davis (on his bike). Quite why Mike was on his bike I don't recall. We all met up at the Shell Garage in Stanley at six-thirty in the morning. It was barely light and dogs were still barking as we set off towards the main Island Road by the roundabout above Hairpin Beach. I recall we suffered a moment of mutual indecision as to whether to proceed clockwise, as planned, or change plan and head the other way towards Tai Tam. We turned left and began the slow trudge uphill towards Chung Hom Kok. It was light now but a grey, muggy day, not cold and not hot. In fact weather wise it was a perfect day for this sort of madness. We passed Repulse Bay, Deep Water Bay, Aberdeen and then 'Pok Fulham.' My feet started to hurt a lot. The decision to 'break in' new shoes that day was not a good one. The road followed the contours of quite high ground as we started to head north around the clock so to speak. If the walk was indeed a clock then we were probably at about ten on the dial and the time was about eleven. Mike had been pushing his bike (uphill) most of the way and he would have been better off without it. By twelve noon we were into the Mid-Levels area and to our surprise Mike bade us farewell as he free wheeled downhill into Conduit Road where he lived. We were down to five. Our route planning had included a pit stop at the much loved China Fleet Club which was owned and operated by the Royal Navy. In those days, before land reclamation, it was actually on the waterfront opposite the Police Head Quarters and on the very edge of Wan Chai, the epicentre of the 'Girlie Bar' land of Suzie Wong. Our fathers were all Honorary Associate Members so admission was automatic. To add to my credentials (if I needed them) my paternal grandfather, Clement, was President of the Mess there in 1910 but the records were highly unlikely to have survived the Japanese occupation. Not that 'Pops' was there then. In 1915 all major units had been withdrawn to Europe and he arrived in time for the Gallipoli Campaign, Jutland et al.

There were two restaurants in the 'Fleet Club' for Officers and Other Ranks respectively. We knew our place in life – and lunched in the Officer's Mess! We all five ate chicken curry OTB (off the bone), apple pie á la mode (with ice cream) and a pint of draught San Miguel beer. We decided, wisely, to stick to a single beer. When we left about an hour later, probably about one 'o' clock, we walked up Arsenal Street to join the main road heading due east. For some reason at this juncture Steve decided he'd had enough and jumped on a No. 6 bus for Stanley outside Victoria Barracks.

Now we were four. We trudged on at about two knots towards Causeway Bay and North Point, roughly following the tram lines. Disaster struck as a heel came off my brand new shoe! Very fortunately small street side cobblers were plentiful and cheap and a ten minutes and five bucks later we were on our way again. Reaching Shau Ki Wan and a fork in the road we turned uphill, in fact a very steep hill. I think it was Benjie who said:

'Why the heck are we going this way? Let's stick to the flatter road although it might be a bit further.'

'No, there's a reason we're going this way. Trust me.'

About fifteen minutes later we stopped outside a huge, green imposing building that looked a bit like a church. I rang the bell and seconds later an Italian gentlemen wearing black robes and a tight white collar opened the huge door. Welcome to the Salesian School.

'Good afternoon. Can I 'elp you?'

Father Cavalin was such a nice man and it took a little while for him to remember me as Father Christmas's boy! Paddy was fortunately in residence and was summoned to come down from somewhere several levels away. He was stunned to see me but delighted. He shook hands with us all as I introduced him to Benjie, Andrew and Geoffrey. We were ushered into a small hospitality room and soon cakes and Cokes arrived with a member of staff.

'And so tell me, Mark, you've all walked from Stanley so...'

'Yes, Paddy, clockwise, the long way round.'

'Goodness me! You'll be needing a proper drink then I'll...'

'No thanks really. Coke is just fine. Thank you.'

I knew what Paddy had meant. He sometimes joined as at home for roast beef and Yorkshire Puddings – plus a half a bottle of Jamesons on the balcony with Dad afterwards. What a lovely man he was. After a rest of about half an hour we set off on the last leg – about six miles. There was still about an other mile of ''uphill' and a fine misty rain was falling but it was quite welcome in a funny sort of way. We reached the summit by the turn off to Big Wave Bay and turned downhill towards Tai Tam reservoir which we could see about two miles distant. At least it was downhill now and our spirits rose. We reached the road over the dam and crossed in single file, quite smartly in case a No.14 Bus decided to prematurely end the day's event. Three miles to go. The light was fading so it was maybe about six 'o' clock. An Army Land Rover coming from behind us slowed down to walking speed as it drew level. It was some squaddies from the Duke of Wellington's at Stanley Fort. We declined offers of a lift and they were in total disbelief when we told them we had left Stanley at first light that morning. A mile later with the light fading fast and with only another to go a green Cortina flashed its lights at us. It was Dad doing a recce to see how we were doing. By the time we reached the Shell garage and parted company all pain in my feet had disappeared as they were by now totally numb. We had done it! To mark the achievement Dad marked our four names in black ink on the base of his cribbage board. High praise indeed.

After Easter the weather started to warm up again and with the beach and the Yacht Club, not to mention the bowling green providing permanent distractions, life in a textbook did not have many attractions. At least I now only had four subjects left and I was broadly optimistic.

I did get one heck of a surprise one day after school though. It was a Monday and the tea table was only set for three. Where was Dad?

'Your father wasn't allowed to tell us until today but he has gone to Okinawa for the week.'

What the heck! In later years when I took up writing, I thought that *'Gone to Okinawa'* was a great title for a book. God knows what I would write about but the title was great. The following Sunday Dad returned in one piece having being picked up, once again, by 'Admiral Bradshaw' but whether five bucks tea money was involved that time I don't know. He'd flown by NorthWest Orient Airlines (the fan jet airline according to their ads) to Naha, Okinawa with a colleague from the RAAF and they had spent the week courtesy of the US Air Force and the National Security Agency at an international intelligence conference. He came back with tales of noisy B52 bombers, American beer and wonderful hospitality. He also brought back a souvenir in the shape of a dark blue glass fish ornament. In WW2 casualties had been high on both sides and many field hospitals had been set up that used thousands of dark blue medicine bottles. Over the years these bottles had been recycled into ornaments by entrepreneurial locals. That's what I was told anyway and I have no reason to disbelieve it. By the way, I still have the fish. That trip, with his Australian colleague whose name I know but will not mention, was evidence of the UKUSA Treaty signed in 1946 and which even pre- dated NATO. It ensured all countries party to the Treaty automatic access to received signals intelligence from the other parties. In the late Sixties the Peoples Republic of China was an unknown quantity. Enough said.

Speaking of Okinawa, an archipelago twixt Hong Kong and Japan, it reminds me of a wonderful Radio Hong Kong presenter called Bob Williams who was becoming quite prominent in his field. Bob hosted a show called 'Bumper to Bumper' every weekday between five and six. It was assumed that many listeners would be in their cars and stuck in traffic jams on the way home. Hence the title of the programme. I never met Bob but Dad did as he was an associate of Frank Rees. He was a Canadian and serving in the Marines had lost a leg during the invasion of Okinawa. Dad recorded many of his shows in the early Seventies on the new, all singing, all dancing system known as cassette recorders and I am pleased to say that several of them are still in my possession. Bob was a legend and was to Radio Hong Kong what say David Jacobs was to Radio Two. They just don't make 'em like that any more.

The time just flew by and before we knew it the 'O' level season was upon us. So was the typhoon season but fortunately they stayed well south. They usually do until about August as Shirley had proved the year before. French 'O' level was split into two separate exams – written and oral. I remember nothing about the former and everything bout the latter. London University flew a female examiner to Hong Kong in early June to conduct the oral exams, probably at two or three schools that followed the London Board curriculum. The great day arrived and one by one, about every twenty minutes, we were called by name by the examiner into a small interview room. I was about half way down the list of maybe a dozen candidates.

'Monsieur 'arland, bonjour. Je m'appelle Mademoiselle de Gaulle' (or whatever her name was). 'Assezey vous, s'il vous plaît.'

Although English, she was obviously in character straight away so I went along with it. Why not? The room was not air conditioned, a lone ceiling fan brought only minimal relief. I was already sweating like a dingo's crutch, as Bruce Denham might have said on the bowling green.

'Sacré bleu! C'est très chaud aujourdh'ui Mademoiselle, n'est-ce pas?'

'Vous avez raison, absolument.'

And that bit of banter set the tone for the whole, very short oral exam. I was out in less than ten minutes but as I was leaving the room she lapsed into English and said:

'I can't decide whether you have a very good French accent or you are just a good mimic.'

'Quelle différence?

She shrugged her shoulders. It was almost three months before I learnt that I had passed with a Grade A. The others would not be so simple as I was soon to discover. The Geography was easy peasy, the written French very tricky, the Chemistry and Physics both OK but the Additional Maths (Greek calculus posing as maths) impossible. Latin (for which I sat a CSE in the hope of obtaining a Grade 1 equivalent to an 'O' level) was sadly not to deliver a satisfactory battle honour and I 'fell in a foreign field' so to speak, eight thousand miles away from either Roma or Londinium. I should have taken note of that hand written inscription in that first textbook 'Latin is a language as dead as dead can be etcetera.' At least I learnt something.

It was now the end of June, exams were over and even Peter Sarstedt 's *Where do you go to my lovely*' was off the number one spot in the charts. It seemed to have been there for ever, certainly through all the long weeks of revision. Thoughts turned to the journey home at the end of July, or should I say to the UK? Home was where you made it now and Clifford T. Ward's lovely *Home thoughts from abroad* hadn't even been written. *In a Gadda da Vidda* and *Soul Finger* from the Bar Kays jostled for the most play time on Commercial Radio.

Pass or fail the exams the official school timetable was effectively over for us. John Kotch was still teaching at St. Georges and once again as our Form Teacher he organised two very different and contrasting trips for us. The first one was to the studios of Rediffusion TV which was just a few hundred yards away. It was really interesting and we saw the 'hot seat' where the newsreaders sat and the weather girls spoke about 'early morning Miss' in Tokyo. We even saw the Colony's most popular newsreader, Tony Fry, a suave good looking dude in his late twenties. All the girls swooned over him like flies round a jam jar. Tarts! Sandra in particular appeared even more flush than usual as her hormones got caught up in a jetstream. Neither Sandra, Mike nor myself could possibly have imagined that a month later Tony would be on the same P & O liner, *Orsova*, for the voyage home. That is another story that must be told.

The second trip away from school could not have been in greater contrast. It was a visit to a leper colony. Yes you did read that correctly, a leper colony. Some kids backed out and Mr Kotch did not take offence. The colony itself was located on an island in the South China Sea a few miles east of Silver Mine Bay, Lantau Island. As you might imagine, there was no public ferry service. I am not sure if that was to deter curious visitors or to discourage the inmates from leaving the island. It was called Hei Ling Chau and probably covered about a half a square mile. We were conveyed there courtesy of the Royal Navy and I think it might have been the same tender that took us to Stonecutters Island almost a year earlier. It took an hour to get there but it was a pleasant day and not too hot if I remember rightly. We were well briefed before our arrival and were told that there was absolutely no risk whatsoever of catching leprosy. It was a common myth that if you touched a leper then you became one yourself. The movie *Ben Hur* had done nothing to dispel that misconception. So with the boat's engines slowing down we gently glided into a basin and tied up at a long wooden jetty. A Chinese chap dressed in whites, a Dr Somebody, welcomed us to Hei Ling Chau and we disembarked. We were offered cold drinks from a tray which was held before us by a chap with no hands and stunted arms. That was just the opening batsman. Over the course of the next few hours we toured the island which was remarkably self sufficient in water, vegetables and fish. It was the clinic and hospital suites that got to you. Colin (Ay-Uggs) Smith fainted when a chap with half a face missing appeared. Unbelievably one of the Chinese guides had a command of English which allowed him to tell two jokes:

'Those guys over there playing Chinese checkers used to play poker – but one of them kept throwing his hand in. And see those pretty girls over there? They used to be prostitutes but business kept falling off.'

You couldn't make it up. Lunch was provided for us in a refectory of westernised Chinese food like spring rolls and fried rice. Plain, simple but adequate. None of us had much of an appetite. Not surprising really when you think about it. I think we were all relieved when it was time to sail back to Hong Kong Island. It was just as well the Navy came back for us. You would not want to be stranded there for all the tea in China. It was a difficult day to take in but I was glad I went. How many people can honestly say they have been to a Leper Colony? Not many. Not even Charlton Heston I'll wager.

CHAPTER 19

A part from the delicious prawns consumed in great quantities on Lantau Island I haven't really mentioned food but it is a topic that cannot go without mention. Our very first Chinese meal was in fact taken at the Lucky Dragon Chinese Restaurant in Scarborough on my 13th birthday exactly one week before we sailed from London on the *Bendoran*. We were staying in the Victoria Hotel who's only claim to fame to be frank was that it was the birthplace of Charles Laughton the actor in *Mutiny on the Bounty* and *I, Claudius*. The Lucky Dragon was Scarborough's first Chinese restaurant. It was also our first experimentation with chopsticks, much to the amusement of the staff. In the weeks that followed aboard *Bendoran* the largely Chinese galley crew treated us to Cantonese cuisine every few days but it was fairly tame to meet the palates, we suspected, of the mainly Scottish and Hebridean officers and cadets. It wasn't exactly sweet and sour haggis but there was nothing too exotic or untoward. So our first proper Chinese meal in Hong Kong was a revelation and if my memory serves me correctly was at the Nam Ah restaurant in Happy Valley amidst the sea of shoe shops I mentioned earlier. We went there on the personal recommendation of Frank Rees, a self-confessed 'foodie' and restaurant junkie. If he were alive today he would be in his absolute element on Trip Advisor.

It was a Saturday night and the drive in from Stanley was mercifully uneventful. Dad didn't flood the Cortina's carburettor and we managed to get parked not far from the Lee Theatre which was only a few minutes walk away. On arrival we were immediately shown upstairs and we found several other 'Gweilo' families already enjoying the evening. Beers were ordered, for Dad at least, and probably 7UP or Coke for everyone else. Menus were also brought to us. Big problem. They were all in Chinese. Fortunately an English speaking waiter arrived and introduced himself.

'You frien of Mr Lees? He my frien also. Welcome. I giff you wha Mr Lees always haff? OK?'

We went along with this to keep things simple. The food was extraordinarily good I do remember, the highlight being Vietnamese blue crabs in a black bean sauce. Whether the imminent arrival of all out war in Vietnam interrupted the availability of these Indo-Chinese crustaceans I don't know. Apart from the taste the memorable feature was the way they were served at the table being wrapped in tea towels and then hit with a mallet to crush the shells.

It was the first of many memorable outings for local cuisines but as Hong Kong was such a cosmopolitan city you could take your pick of virtually whatever kind of food you fancied. There was the Australian Café for steaks (peculiarly served with hot toast and Anchor butter), Maxims of Paris, The Café de Milan, the San Francisco Steakhouse, the Koreana which served Korean food which you mainly cooked yourself on a charcoal burner at the table and for me the best of all was the Indonesian Restaurant just around the corner from the Sunning House Hotel in Causeway Bay. The 'prawns sambal' and 'nasi goreng' (a peppery fried rice) were just sensational but were very hot indeed to the uninitiated palate. Be warned.

As you might expect with the Colony being surrounded by the warm waters of the South China Sea the seafood was excellent and varied. We were indeed fortunate that Stanley Market had a fish section where we would regularly buy a katty of delicious prawns, particularly if Mum was making a home made curry. The garoupa too was delicious and plentiful and was chopped like steaks through the starfish shaped bone in the centre. With Macau only forty miles west the Portuguese influence was ever present and 'garoupa á la Portuguese' which was cooked with much hot peppers and tomatoes was a favourite. I said earlier that politically speaking Macau was a different kettle of fish which brings to mind perhaps the best thing ever to come out of that enclave – the Macau sole. I do not know enough about the generic classification of flatfish to amplify on family, genus or species but all I can tell you is that the Macau sole is simply divine. Just think of Dover sole, discard cold Channel waters and the Forecast for Shipping from your mind and dream. Add a generous drizzle of melted garlic butter, a few green beans, a sprig of parsley and a gallon of cold San Mig and there you have it. The best Macau sole was served in the China Fleet Club. Many years later, in the early Nineties, I took an elderly Chinese businessman and retired Army General, Alex K.H. Hsu, to lunch there and he told me it was the best Macau sole he had ever tasted. Praise indeed.

We must have sampled over a hundred Chinese restaurants over three years, mostly based on personal recommendations and in this respect the Prison Officers from Stanley were a mine of information and good advice. This was particularly the case of our bowling friend, Mr Belwant 'B' Singh who had been in the Colony since time immemorial and who was bilingual. I'd noticed that whenever he was supervising the prisoners rolling the bowling green an instruction to them in Cantonese was always met with the same disdainful reply of 'Dew lei lo mo!' So it was to B whom I turned to solve the mystery. It seemed to be a ubiquitous and almost casual response. B's reply was a bit of a shocker.

'It means go and fornicate with your mother!' Better be careful who you say that to I thought at the time. I soon learnt that the Chinese had derogatory names and terms for most other races and creeds and that in reality they were the most racist people on earth. Apart from calling us 'Gweilos' (foreign devils) they reserved a particularly nasty phrase for anyone coming from the Indian sub-continent which at the time was the whole of India, West and East Pakistan (now Bangladesh) and that was the 'Yan Do Yan' – the Dirty People. Charming, I'm sure. This brings me back to Sikhs who I mentioned earlier in connection with the temple. Occasionally on a Saturday morning Dad and I would drive into town from Stanley and park in the Hilton Hotel car park, perhaps before we went into the Head Office of the Hongkong & Shanghai Banking Corporation which was conveniently close by. I was bemused by the fact that the Sikh shroff (what a lovely word) would give us a salute, a smile and a wave as he raised the barrier to let us in. With his whiskers, yellow turban and uniform (but minus a blunderbuss) he looked every inch a watchman on the Khyber Pass. What mystified me was the parking charges were normally very high but we never seemed to pay a bean, or even a grain of rice. The explanation from Dad was a revelation and went something like this:

'Mr Singh (another one) is a Sikh and because he's not Chinese his employers don't give him the traditional double money at Chinese New Year. That's not fair on him. So, a load of us at Sai Wan club together and pay him a wad in cash to make up for it. In turn he let's us in for free. It probably adds up to a lot more than his monthly salary as well. So we all win, except his employers who discriminate against him because of his race. See?'

I did indeed and it was yet another lesson learnt in how to oil the wheels of commerce. Twenty years later I put it into practice myself in a Scarborough car park where the underpaid and genial attendant was fond of a drop of Glenfiddich at Christmas, a litre of which was a lot cheaper than a pound a day – plus VAT over a whole year. The things you learnt as a teenager in the British Empire!

After a coffee and a cake in the Cat Street Café which was part of the Hilton complex we indeed often did venture into the HK & Shanghai Bank at No. 1 Queen's Road, Central. It was air conditioned and in the summer months was marvellous to walk into for a cooling few minutes. While Dad cashed a cheque (no ATMs in those days although they were developed in Hong Kong) I would stare and admire the stunning frescos on walls and ceilings that depicted the history of Hong Kong from its origins in the 1840s right through to its international trading status today. Sadly in the 1980s, when the building was demolished to make way for the megalith we know today, those frescos could not be saved. All that was saved were two stone lions outside the front entrance on Des Voeux Road, which in true 'feng shui' practice guarded people's wealth from all would-be thieves. It must have worked as when the replacement edifice was constructed the two lions were not allowed to be moved one inch during the two year project. Was that blind faith or silly superstition. It amused me greatly when the muesli-munching new world trendies of later decades adopted 'feng shui' as an alternative take on life, design and ambience. Millions were made in books, TV shows, DVDs and personal advising. Arranging mirrors, flowers and fish tanks was one thing but if the new believers followed its teachings to the nth degree then buckets of pig's entrails left by a front door would soon, I suspect, cause the dollars to dry up.

My memoires would not be complete without further mention of the Hongkong and Shanghai Banking Corporation known colloquially as the 'Honkers & Shankers' or on the HK Stock Exchange simply 'Hong Kong Bank'. Incorporated in the Colony in 1866 it is one of the oldest 'Hongs' (companies) still trading today. Folklore has it that the 'Tai Pan' (chief executive) of the bank was the second most powerful man in the Colony second only to His Excellency the Governor himself. The founder was a Scot and successive Tai Pans have jealously guarded HSBC as a preserve of their own. If you want to know more about these early bankers and traders then read James Clavell's wonderful novel *'Tai Pan'* which he wrote before *Noble House*.

CHAPTER 20

With two weeks to go before our departure it started to hit home hard that soon our three year tour would be at an end. We started to plan for the voyage back to England. We had known for a year exactly what the timetable was. Departing on 30th July the P & O liner s.s. *Orsova* was to take us to Japan, across the Pacific via Hawaii and California to Vancouver from where we would take the Canadian Pacific Railroad to Montreal and then another ship, the *Empress of England*, to Liverpool. We would depart Hong Kong on 30th July and arrive somewhere near the Liver Building on 10th September. Wow. Our car, the now highly favoured Ford Cortina, would also be returning to the UK. It had sailed east with us on the *Bendoran* but paradoxically it would be hold cargo on the s.s. *Neleus* of the Blue Funnel Line and a great competitor of the Ben Line. She too would sail to Liverpool about a week after our departure and, hopefully, would arrive in Liverpool just before us.

The reality was that a major commercial catastrophe had affected that sector of the British Merchant Marine that traded with the Far East. In June 1967 Israel and Egypt fought each other in what became known as the 'Six Day War' and resulted in the Suez Canal being closed for years. With the Canal being deliberately closed at both ends by ships sunk by the Egyptians there was no escape for the dozen or more merchant vessels stuck in the middle in the Bitter Lakes. The corrosive effect of the desert sands took its toll and the ships became known as the 'Yellow Fleet.' The Ben Line was lucky with all its vessels being outside the war zone when war broke out but the Blue Funnel Line was not so fortunate. The *Agapenor* and the *Melampus* were trapped for years and a liability, not a profit centre, for their owners the Liverpool based Alfred Holt.

Both Lines' ships were designed and built from the outset for the Far East run via the Canal and they would race full tilt for Aden to bunker, just as we had done. Many records were broken on this run as speed and delivery made money. With the Canal closed the longer, slower detour via South Africa and the Cape of Good Hope completely altered the economics. It was the beginning of the end. Scaling down, mergers and finally containerisation all took their toll of those two great British companies, one English one Scottish, that for a century had fed and accelerated the most rampant Tiger economy on earth – Hong Kong.

The shipping agent from Blue Funnel would not come to collect the Cortina until our very last day in Stanley. In fact we left it in the Gordon Terrace car park with the keys at our neighbours, the Claytons. We had a final few shopping trips to the NAAFI at Stanley Fort to buy a few more items at cheap and duty free prices while we still could. Some more LPs were purchased for our collection including Acker Bilk's Greatest Hits and Chris Barber, my Dad's favourite. Oh yes, and some more tins of St. Juliens tobacco to secrete into the household effects.

There was a moment of panic when with a week to go we suddenly realised that I did not own a suit. P & O were sticklers for rules and a suit was compulsory attire for dining in First Class. To the rescue came 'Shanghai Tom Tailor' a Stanley based bespoke outfitters fortunately on the main road to St. Stephens Beach. The cost was HK$200 with an extra ten percent bonus for completing the job in time. It was navy blue and fitted like a glove. If you think the passengers had to be 'tarted up' then spare a thought for the officers who had to wear ceremonial 'whites' and carry a dress sword. On reflection I think I must put those memories onto paper soon as well.

Mum and Linda went to town on a few shopping sprees as well although the 'must have' purchase of the world renowned Mikimoto pearls from the fabulous Lane Crawford department store had been effected the previous Christmas. Needless to say the Christmas tree was already packed and unbelievably was still in use after the millennium. Extra boxes of brass screws were purchased from the Mai Tai Kee hardware store in Stanley and in the gardening department several score of bamboo canes (for growing runner beans) were acquired.

With Mike and a few others from school I went to my last 'disco night' at the United Services Recreation Club (the USRC) in Kowloon which had become a regular Saturday night out. At almost sixteen we were, after all, adults now weren't we? I had my last smooch with a lovely girl called Rona Smith to the sound of *San Franciscan Nights* by Eric Burden and the Animals, an anti-war song written and sung long before *'Where have all the flowers gone?'* Check it out for yourself on YouTube and try and keep a dry eye. I can't. I had made many friends at the USRC mainly from King George the Fifth School where that taxi had mistakenly taken us when Dad confused Wellington with Waterloo. So on that warm Kowloon night (as well as San Franciscan) it was goodbye to Rona, Barbara Ross, Sally Baylis, Maureen

Grindlay, Pamela Apps and the Kiwi, Lynette Taylor. I hope you are all alive and well and maybe get to read this little book.

CHAPTER 21

It was July 16th and I remember it well for two reasons. It was my sixteenth birthday and, if all went well, a momentous day for three Americans on the other side of the International Date Line at Cape Canaveral in Florida. Now let me see, was it Wednesday or Monday over there if it was Tuesday here? 'As you go west, a day goes west' rang through my mind. Anyway, whatever, it was the start of a four day journey that, God willing, would end in the greatest leap for mankind, its first step on the Moon. Although we still had the TV switched on our flat was in utter chaos as we sorted out the furniture to be staying there in the flat, the furniture we were shipping back to UK and the quality rosewood furniture we were buying from Mr Frank Wilkes of DOLFRA. Remember him? As arranged Frank came round, without Dolly (I always think of that cloned sheep) to negotiate a price for a job lot. As an amiable chap who liked a 'wet' whether the sun was over the yardarm or not, Dad was very liberal with the drinks poured from behind the very realistic rosewood bar common to all the flats in Gordon Terrace. I can't remember what his tipple was but whatever Dad showered triples of it in Frank's direction in the hope of a nice low price. The final price was a straight $1,000 but I heard later that this was just pantomime on his part and the price was always $1,000 whatever you bought from him. The TV wasn't too exciting because there were no visuals, just live commentary from the Voice of America... five, four, three, two, one....ignition...yes sir...we have lift-off at whatever time it was Eastern Daylight Time.' A short time after that Dolly arrived in an expensive car to pick Frank up. Renting furniture was good business it seemed.

For the next few days we continued to empty the flat and were looking forward to spending the last few days in Hong Kong in a nice hotel, in our case the Ambassador in Nathan Road, Kowloon which was only a short distance from the Ocean Terminal. We had a mild scare round about the 20th when a severe earth tremor hit southern Guandong Province which of course ignored political boundaries and rumbled Hong Kong too. It woke me up at about six in the morning as it sounded like a train coming. I saw the light fitting in my bedroom swaying and I thought, oh heck we're almost ready to leave after three years and it's all going to end in a huge pile of rubble, sniffer dogs and body bags. It lasted about five seconds which seemed like an age. Suddenly it stopped and the light ceased to sway. Thank you, Mr Richter, for a low score that day. Next day's papers however barely gave it a mention with the moon landing itself taking precedence over all other news.

On our last weekend in Stanley Dad played his last game of bowls at the Stanley Club and it would be another three years before he played there again. It proved a pleasant watering hole in the evenings too, not just for Prison Officers but for others like my Dad and his colleagues who liked a jar and a chat and you might say that in this respect it served the same function as the hundreds of Red Lions and Dog and Ducks back in England. The Officer Commanding the local garrison was also I seem to remember made an

Honorary member of the Club whichever Regiment was based at Stanley Fort. In the early to mid Seventies I was a student at the now defunct Oxford Polytechnic and Mum and Dad were once again back serving in Hong Kong. We exchanged weekly 'Air Mail Blueys' and one day Dad, in his letter, wrote something like this:

'I had the oddest conversation in the Club bar a couple of days ago, I think he was the CO of the Black Watch up at the Fort. He'd had a few but he told me that he'd been told that day that the MOD (Ministry of Defence) had already decided that the Black Watch would be the last British Army unit to be stationed in Hong Kong and that if their two blokes were still banged up in prison they were to spring them hours before the Handover rather than leave them behind. What do you make of that?!'

It was indeed a most peculiar tale but it had a ring of realism behind it. A few years earlier two Black Watch Guardsmen had been convicted of murdering taxi drivers in two entirely separate incidents. They both pleaded alcoholic amnesia but were charged, found guilty and were both sentenced to death, capital punishment still being in force in the Colony. The Governor commuted their sentences to life imprisonment and they were incarcerated, I believe at Stanley. The Handover was still twenty years away. The conversation and Dad's letter were forgotten.

Anyway, back to the timeline. On the day we left Stanley, I think the 25th July, one car and one mini- van took us, with no less than eighteen pieces of baggage, first to the vehicular ferry at North Point and then to the Ambassador Hotel. I don't think our driver parted with five bucks. We had an evening meal at the YMCA which was always a pleasant spot for a bite to eat. Still having a few days to kill before sailing we visited a few places and shops that we would not normally have bothered to journey to from Stanley. The last major treat though was to take 'Afternoon Tea' at the splendid Peninsula Hotel. Sipping the finest Earl Grey and munching cakes and tiny sandwiches accompanied by a string quartet on a minstrel's gallery was something to behold. Little wonder that General Tanaka, the occupying commander of the Imperial Japanese Army, had made 'The Pen' his HQ. I took numerous walks in the vicinity of the Clock Tower which was an imposing structure of brick and granite. It marked the entrance to the Kowloon Canton Railway station and it was easy to forget that back in 1913, when it was built, hardly anybody could have afforded to own a timepiece. The clock tower thus wasn't just a landmark but a necessity. A hundred years later it is the only reminder that this was the railway terminus for a slow train to China which I guess made a change from a slow boat.

We were due to sail on the 30th but nature intervened with the tail end of a Tropical Storm in the South China Sea which delayed the arrival of *Orsova* into the Fragrant Harbour by a whole day. With my classmates Mike Davis and Sandra Coupland also departing on the same ship, not to mention sixth formers Carl Olsen, Tony Lyth and John Stanton, we had accumulated loads of boarding passes to give to friends. You can't beat P & O for ritual, formality and tradition. A full Ghurkha band played *A Life on the Ocean Wave, Sunset* and *Rule Britannia* as the streamers and bunting stretched between the ship and shore finally snapped one at a time.

My 'Thousand days in Hong Kong' had come to an end.

* * *

POSTSCRIPT

This might surprise you but this is the hardest part of the book to write. How do you sum up, let alone follow up, a thousand days in the most exhilarating place on earth? I returned to Hong Kong many times in later years to live, work and play. Although exciting, it never matched those days in the Nineteen Sixties for sheer magic. Maybe that's because I was at 'that age' when things that happen to you set a pattern or a template for later life.

I learnt a lot, not just at St Georges School, but about the world. My decision not to attend a boarding school in England but to go to a British Army School on the other side of the world had been the right choice to make. I went to six schools between the ages of five and eighteen in three separate countries and St Georges was the best. I am sure that many of my former fellow pupils will echo that sentiment. It wasn't just the schooling, which was first class, but the huge advantage of that education taking place in the most vibrant and commercially successful city on earth. That was the icing on the educational cake.

I have no time for the bleeding heart liberal apologists for the British Empire, the one that made Rome's look like a Minor County. Think of those men, and women, who left the murk of Edinburgh, Liverpool and London, turned east and built the richest jewel in that Empire. Many died in that process, the cholera cemetery at Happy Valley is ample testament to that.

Take five minutes of your time to Google 'Governors of Hong Kong' and you are in for a lesson, not just in history, but of the Empire itself. Some never even set foot in England being servants of the Crown in its Colonies, Protectorates and Dependencies all their lives. It will also reveal where the names of those two boats in Lantau were derived. The *Sir Cecil Clementi* and the *Alexander Grantham* were both former Governors in a bygone age. And as for Des Voeux Road, Stubbs Road and Hennessy Road well they were all named after former Governors too. I'll be lucky to get a ship named after me even allowing for the prefix M.V.

Today 'my Hong Kong' is no more. It is still there of course but now exists as a Special Administrative Region of China. The Chinese government reneged on the Treaty of Nanking. My Hong Kong died on the 30th June 1997 with the Handover to the Communists. Many of us ex-Hong Kongers got together on that dreadful day and tuned in live to the ceremony on TV.

As the ceremonial countdown to midnight started some goose stepping goons of the People's Liberation Army raised the Chinese flag as the Union Jack was reverently lowered for the last time by an Honour Guard of the Black Watch. My father turned to me and said:

'Oh my God, do you remember that conversation I told you about all those years ago in the bar of the Stanley Club?'

Later that evening more than twenty of us banqueted at the Hong Kong restaurant in Scarborough. The proprietor, sadly no longer with us, was Paul Tam a former resident of Sheung Shui in the New Territories. He did us proud that night with complimentary bottles of brandy on the table. The toast, at ten 'o' clock, was to Her Majesty the Queen.

Just a few years ago I was listening to the Zoe Ball Show on Radio 2 and in particular the Saturday morning feature known as Teenage Kicks. Listeners are invited to choose three tunes that reminded them of their teenage years and the reasoning for their choice. I texted the presenter with my selection expecting to hear no more of it. Two days later I was stunned to receive a call from the programme producer at Broadcasting House in London.

'Hi, I'm pleased to tell you that your name and selection has been chosen. You're on next Saturday morning but please, can you just clarify that tune *In a Gadda da Vida*? Is it really seventeen minutes long?'

I set my alarm for six-thirty to make sure I didn't miss it. As I listened to the Kinks' *Waterloo Sunset* to remind me of St. Georges on Waterloo Road, the Doors' *Light my Fire* to remind me of the squaddies of the Duke of Wellington's Regiment listening to the juke box at The Shack and finally the simply amazing *In a Gadda da Vida* from the American band Iron Butterfly, my imagination, not to mention the music, took me back to a different time in a different place.

It was said by many that Hong Kong was a freak of history, geography and politics – a borrowed place on borrowed time. Well maybe it was but it was also built from nothing in a little over a hundred years. So whether you were a soldier, sailor, pilot, builder, entrepreneur, policeman or prison officer and however small or large your contribution and whatever your race, religion or creed, I raise my glass to you all. Yam sing, pang yau! Cheers my friend.

On the tenth anniversary of the Handover, in 2007, a Notice was published in the 'In Memoriam' column of the *Daily Telegraph*. The much lamented loss was for the British

Crown Colony of Hong Kong. There was much speculation at the time as to who had posted the Notice. A former Governor perhaps or a Tai Pan? For the first time I can now reveal who it was. It was me.

In memoriam

HONG KONG.—June 30th 1997 The ultimate take-away R.I.P

Online ref: 14614

****